How to Use the Guide

The fold-out map at the beginning of each volume provides an overview of all the sites in the region, with quick links, emergency contacts and other handy information. The text is arranged by town, from southwest to northeast. A map of a town or several towns, with numbered and named public access sites, marks the beginning of each section. Site descriptions provide information about what visitors can expect to see or do, GPS coordinates, directions and parking information. Symbols offer a quick visual reference to available facilities, but may not be inclusive of all amenities. Readers can obtain additional information by contacting the managing agency or organization directly or visiting its website (see Resources at the end of the *Guide*).

Facilities Legend

Campground

Floating Dock

Grill

Group Picnic Shelter

Hand-carry Boat Launch

Parking

Picnic Area

Playground

Restrooms

Trailered Boat Launch

Ferry Service

Accessibility for People with Disabilities

The Maine Coastal Program is unable, at this time, to provide complete information about accessibility for all sites in the *Guide*. Readers can obtain more detailed information about access at state properties managed by the Department of Agriculture, Conservation and Forestry's Division of Parks and Public Lands by checking the Division's website, **www.maine.gov/doc/parks** or by calling 207-287-3821. To determine if a site has facilities that meet the needs of the visitor, whether owned by the state, towns or private organizations, readers are advised to contact the property owner or manager (see Resources section).

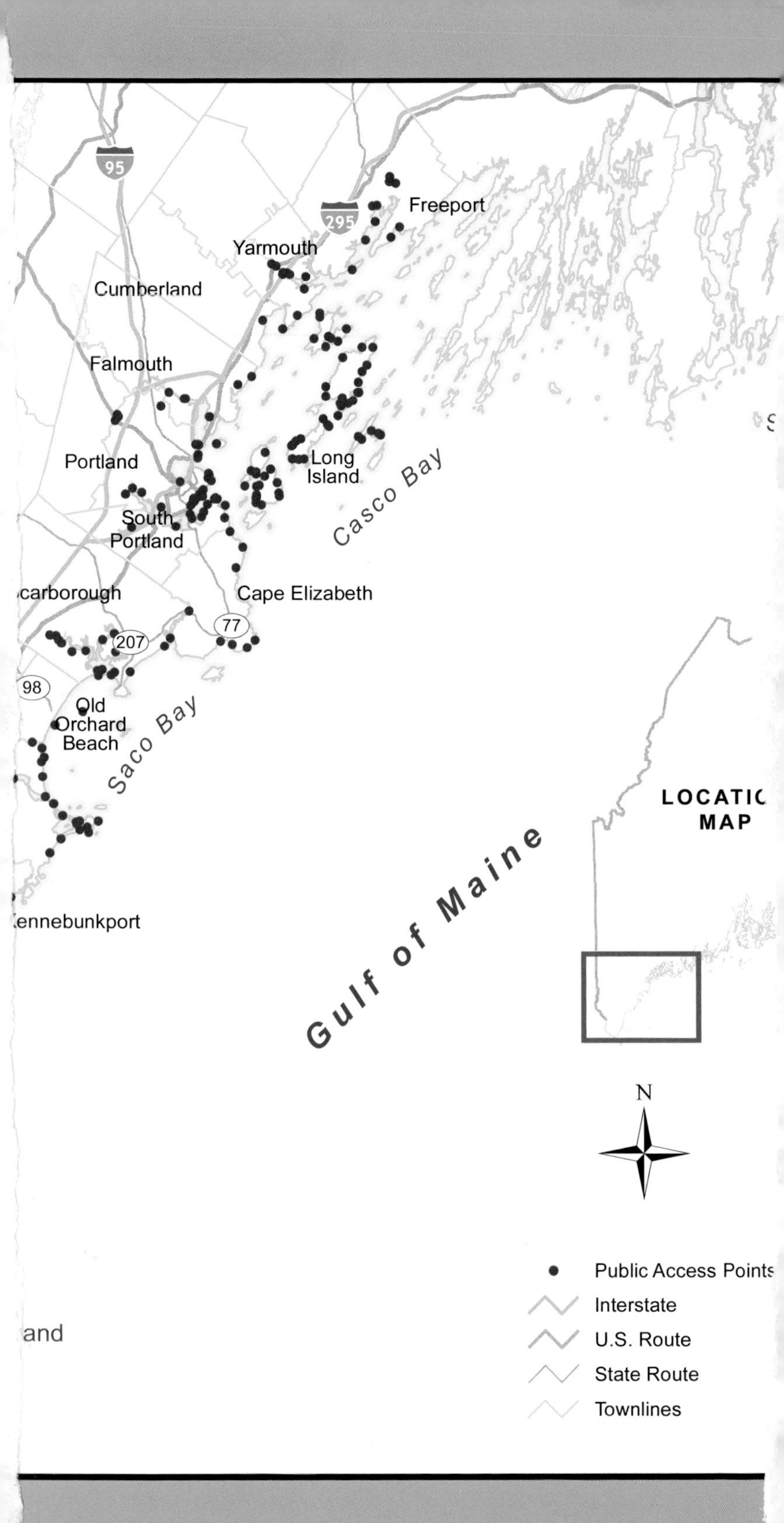
95
295
Freeport
Yarmouth
Cumberland
Falmouth
Portland
Long
Island
Casco Bay
South
Portland
carborough
Cape Elizabeth
77
207
98
Old
Orchard
Beach
Saco Bay
ennebunkport
Gulf of Maine
LOCATIC
MAP
N
Public Access Points
Interstate
U.S. Route
State Route
Townlines
and

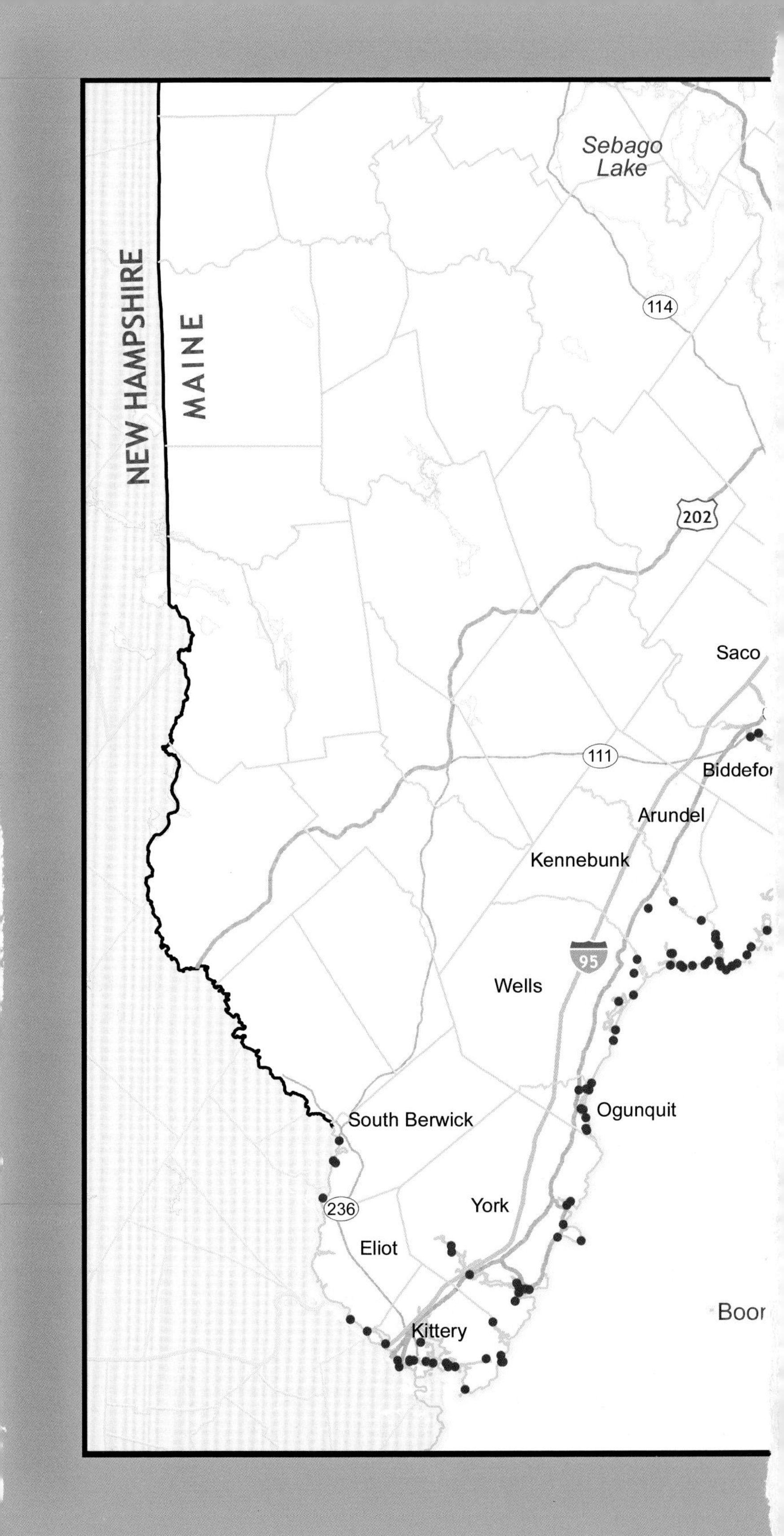

Sebago Lake
NEW HAMPSHIRE
MAINE
114
202
Saco
111
Biddefo
Arundel
Kennebunk
95
Wells
Ogunquit
South Berwick
236
York
Eliot
Boo
Kittery

Leave Your Fire Wood at Home

Fires are not allowed at most sites featured here, but if you are going to a place that does allow them, purchase wood from a source near your destination. Because firewood can harbor exotic insects and diseases, it is critical that it not be transported from outside the state (and Maine law bars bringing in untreated firewood) or moved more than 50 miles within the state. Transporting firewood speeds the movement of destructive insects and pathogens which may then become established at campsites across the state and cause immense damage to adjacent forests.

Registration for Saltwater Fishing, Licenses for Recreational Harvesting of Shellfish or Marine Worms

Saltwater Fishing: Recreational saltwater fishermen are required by Maine law to sign up on the Maine Saltwater Recreational Fishing Registry. There are some exceptions, so to find out who is exempt from registering and/or to register, visit: **www.maine.gov/saltwater** or call 207-633-9505.

Harvesting Shellfish and Marine Worms: Recreational shellfish harvesters must obtain a license from municipalities and there are limits on the amount that can be harvested by recreational fishermen. (See Resources for municipal contact information.) Harvesting of marine worms for personal use is limited to 125 worms per day without a license.

Areas Closed to Harvesting: To protect public health, shellfish harvesting is allowed only in areas classified as "open" by Maine's Department of Marine Resources. In areas designated as open, water quality meets acceptable standards and toxic algae are not present. Please be aware that the status of an area may change from "open" to "closed." For information about closures, check this link: **www.maine.gov/dmr/rm/public_health** or call the Maine Red Tide and Shellfish Sanitation Hotline at 1-800-232-4733 or 207-624-7727. Maps of areas open to harvesting are also available from towns.

For details about how Maine residents can fish for lobster and crabs for personal use, visit **www.maine.gov/dmr/rm/lobster/guide**.

For Your Safety

Consumption Advisory: Chemicals in lobster tomalley and in some Maine saltwater fish may be harmful to humans. Women who are or may become pregnant as well as children are particularly at risk. The Maine Center for Disease Control and Prevention advises that fish is good for you and your family if you follow consumption limits outlined in the Safe Eating Guidelines, available at **www.maine.gov/dhhs/mecdc/environmental-health/eohp/fish.**

Hunting: Hunting is allowed on some properties; visitors to these sites should stay on marked trails and wear blaze orange during hunting season. For more information about Maine hunting seasons visit the Maine Department of Inland Fisheries and Wildlife website at **www.maine.gov/ifw/hunting_trapping** or call 207-287-8000.

Tidal Ranges: Visitors accustomed to tidal ranges of one or two feet found along and south of the mid-Atlantic states may be impressed with Maine tides, which average nine feet in Kittery and increase in size going northeast to 20 or more feet in Eastport. The larger rivers also have noticeable tides. Hikers crossing sand bars and other low-tide features as well as hand-carry boaters should be aware of these ranges and time trips accordingly. Tide charts are available at **www.tidesandcurrents.noaa.gov/tide predictions**.

eguin Island

10 Miles

Southern Region:

South Berwick to Freeport

Years ago, when saltwater farms were common in Southern Maine, farmers harvested marsh grass for fodder and thatch, each village had a landing, and people used boats to travel from place to place. Life was defined by the annual cycle of planting, growth and harvest. That bucolic era has vanished, but water, wind and seasons still shape coastal use, drawing residents and visitors alike.

Although most visitors head for the beaches, Southern Maine has many other prime attractions. Fort Foster in Kittery Point offers designated areas for wind surfers, kayakers and divers as well as walking paths, swimming, and picnicking facilities. The Rachel Carson National Wildlife Refuge and Scarborough Marsh offer superb opportunities for seeing wading birds, shorebirds and salt marsh plants. The Wells National Estuarine Research Reserve – which includes historic Laudholm Farm – offers numerous programs on coasts and estuaries. In Cape Elizabeth, visitors can snap pictures of Maine's oldest lighthouse at Fort Williams Park or visit Two Lights State Park for its dramatic views of Casco Bay from a steep, rocky, often wave-washed shore.

Portland is the state's most populated city and home to a thriving port that supports a working waterfront, tourism, and ferry service to the Casco Bay islands. In South Portland and Portland, a network of paved trails offers endless opportunities for investigating the interface between sea and shore. More adventurous visitors might take a ferry to one of the small islands in Casco Bay and see the sights by bicycle. The islands featured in this book support small year-round communities and offer visitors the opportunity to enjoy a slower pace of life – to wander along coastal roads, take in the scenery and smell the salt air.

Southern Maine is replete with opportunities. Whether you fancy relaxing on the beach or casting for mackerel, scouting for warblers or following fox tracks, hiking a trail or paddling a coastal river, it's time to dust off your gear, pack a lunch and head out for an adventure at one of the many excellent public access sites along the coast!

"Good Visitor" Guidelines

Maine's shoreline is a patchwork of public and private property. When you visit please consider these guidelines, which will enhance your enjoyment and safety, protect the natural areas themselves, contribute toward good landowner relations, and help ensure continued public access in the future.

Respect Private Property

Please respect site boundaries, rules and restrictions noted in the description or posted at the area. Land trust sites featured in the *Guide*, though open to the public, are privately-owned. At some sites in the *Guide*, visitors use a trail across private property to reach a public access site. In still other instances, easements allow some uses but not others. In almost all cases, the areas described here are adjacent to private property on which access is not allowed.

Maine is one of only a few states in which coastal property owners can own land to the mean low tide line. A centuries-old public easement does allow the public to use the intertidal zone – the land between the high and low tide lines – for commercial and recreational "fishing, fowling and navigation." The recreational activities that fall within the scope of the public easement have been the subject of recent litigation. In 2011, for example, the Maine Supreme Judicial Court found that scuba diving falls within the right of navigation. The law may continue to evolve as legal challenges are brought before the courts. For detailed information about public access and use rights on Maine's coast, visit the University of Maine Sea Grant College Program's website: **www.accessingthemainecoast.com.**

Abide by Rules and Guidelines

Because rules vary greatly from area to area, check which activities are allowed at the site before you go. In general:

- Some areas allow pets (although leash policies, time of day and seasonal restrictions may apply) and others do not.
- The use of motorized vehicles may be restricted.
- Most sites limit access and parking after dark.
- On-street and/or off-street parking at some municipal properties may be by permit only; sometimes permits are available only to residents and other times non-residents may purchase a permit. Contact the municipal office for more information.
- Visitors are asked to stay on established trails and "carry in/carry out" (including both their trash and pet waste).

To obtain detailed information about allowable uses, accessible facilities, and rules in areas managed by the Department's Division of Parks and Public Lands, check the Division's website: **www.maine.gov/doc/parks** or call 207-287-3821.

Protect Ecologically Sensitive Areas

Properties with sensitive habitats, flora or fauna may have special guidelines to minimize visitor impacts; please check kiosks at parking areas and trailheads. In addition, please refrain from entering fenced or posted areas, which are either being restored or need long-term protection. At smaller or particularly sensitive sites, parking lots may be sized to accommodate fewer visitors, so if the parking lot is full, practice good stewardship by returning another time. For more information about minimizing or avoiding impacts on sensitive natural resources, visit the Maine Island Trail Association's website: **www.mita.org/trail/lnt.**

STATE OF MAINE
OFFICE OF THE GOVERNOR
1 STATE HOUSE STATION
AUGUSTA, MAINE
04333-0001

PAUL R. LEPAGE
GOVERNOR

Welcome to the Maine coast, one of the most spectacular shorelines in the world.

This is Maine's first-ever *Coastal Public Access Guide*, a compendium of great access points to Maine's over 5,300-mile coastline. Maine residents and visitors can experience a coastline unlike any other – the sandy beaches of southern Maine, the rocky shores of the mid-coast and Acadia, or the dramatic tides and windswept cliffs of the Downeast region.

Coastal lands and waters are home to a wide array of special natural and cultural resources; playing a major role in Maine's economy. Public access to the shore is vital to the survival of some of Maine's most significant commercial and recreational enterprises, including fishing, marine transportation, tourism, boating and wildlife viewing.

Maine Coastal Program staff has identified more than 700 locations along the coast that are accessible to the public. These properties are a mix of federal, state, municipal and publically accessible private lands, including land trust properties.

Production of this *Guide* has involved a wide variety of talented individuals working together to produce an important, ground-breaking publication for the State of Maine. This is the first edition, and the Maine Coastal Program expects to add new sites in the years to come.

We hope you are able to use this resource to improve your experience on Maine's legendary coast. The *Coastal Public Access Guide* can be your map to many very memorable visits to a unique part of Maine.

As we work beside and enjoy the Maine coast, let's make sure we leave it in the best condition possible for those who follow.

Thank you,

Paul R LePage

Paul R. LePage
Governor

Welcome to the *Maine Coastal Public Access Guide!*

Renowned for its natural resources, scenic beauty, and cultural heritage, the Maine coast provides endless recreational opportunities. Stretching almost 5,300 miles from Kittery to Calais, this diverse region has sand and cobble beaches, rocky headlands, islands, bluffs, estuaries, salt marshes and thriving downtown waterfronts. And although most people think of salt water when they think of the coast, the tide affects the Piscataqua, Kennebec and Penobscot Rivers as far inland as South Berwick, Augusta and Bangor.

The Maine Coastal Program at the Maine Department of Agriculture, Conservation and Forestry – with the assistance of the Wells National Estuarine Research Reserve and an extensive network of private and public organizations dedicated to conserving coastal lands – has created this three-volume Guide (for Southern, Midcoast and Downeast regions) to help residents and visitors alike discover these invaluable resources. Each publication provides information about boat launches and landings, beaches, walking and hiking paths, historical sites, nature preserves, public parks, and right-of-ways to the shore.

Together, the three guides cover more than 700 public access points along tidally-influenced waters on lands owned by municipalities, the State of Maine, the federal government and land trusts (private, nonprofit organizations that conserve and manage land, much of it for public use). One hundred thirty municipalities, state and federal agencies and more than 40 private organizations contributed to the series.

About The Maine Coastal Program

The Maine Coastal Program has, since 1978, focused on balancing sound development and conservation of the state's coastal areas. Working with a network of state agencies, regional planning commissions, coastal towns, nonprofit organizations and other entities, we concentrate on priority problems and opportunities such as water access, harbor management, working waterfronts, land use, changing shorelines, and marine debris. We offer assistance and grants to coastal municipalities and regional organizations, prepare studies, draft policies and guidelines, conduct training and workshops, support research and mapping, promote best practices, and help engender coastal stewardship in residents and visitors through outreach programs such as the annual Coastal Cleanup.

The Maine Coastal Program is funded by the National Oceanic and Atmospheric Administration's Office of Ocean and Coastal Resource Management with matching support from the State of Maine. The program is one of 34 federally approved coastal management programs across the United States, created under the Coastal Zone Management Act of 1972

Rogue Waves and Big Surf: Jetties and rocks can be slippery when wet. They are particularly dangerous when big swells or storm waves lure people to the shore. Rogue waves – large, unpredictable waves that strike the shore without warning – can also sweep visitors off their feet and into the ocean. It is imperative that visitors take these risks seriously.

Swimming – Water Quality and Rip Currents: Water quality at some swimming beaches may become compromised from high levels of bacteria from water runoff and other sources, particularly after heavy rains. Many public beaches in Maine are monitored by volunteers and land managers as part of Maine's Healthy Beaches Program. During the swimming season, up-to-date information about the status of monitored beaches can be found on signs at the beach or at **www.mainehealthybeaches.org.**

A rip current is a rapid, narrow band of water that flows away from shore to deeper waters. People caught in a rip current should remain calm and swim parallel to the shore; it is all but impossible to swim against a current this strong. Beach-goers should remember that although some Maine beaches have lifeguards, many do not.

Poison Ivy: Poison ivy can cause a minor rash in some people and serious debilitation in others; even individuals who have not previously reacted can develop symptoms. In any case, it makes sense to avoid poison ivy, whose irritating oils can be transferred to others via shoes, clothing and pet fur. Poison ivy commonly grows as groundcover along hiking and walking paths, but can take the shape of a woody bush or climbing vine. Look for its characteristic three shiny leaflets – two opposite leaflets with a larger middle leaflet – and white berries.

Mosquitoes and Ticks: Mosquitoes and black flies are seasonally prevalent in Maine. West Nile Virus, a potentially serious viral illness transmitted by mosquitoes, was found in Maine in 2001. To protect against mosquitoes – and therefore the virus – use insect repellent, wear appropriate clothing, and avoid being outdoors at dawn or dusk when mosquitoes are most active.

Ticks are most commonly seen in spring and early summer. The highest populations of both deer ticks and wood ticks (also called dog ticks) are found in southern Maine but their ranges are extending north. Deer ticks can carry Lyme disease. To deter ticks, use insect repellent, tuck pant legs into socks, and wear light colored clothing so you can more easily see and remove them. Check for ticks after every visit to a wooded or grassy area. For more information on biting insects and potential illness please visit the Maine Center for Disease Control and Prevention website at **www.maine.gov/dhhs/mecdc.**

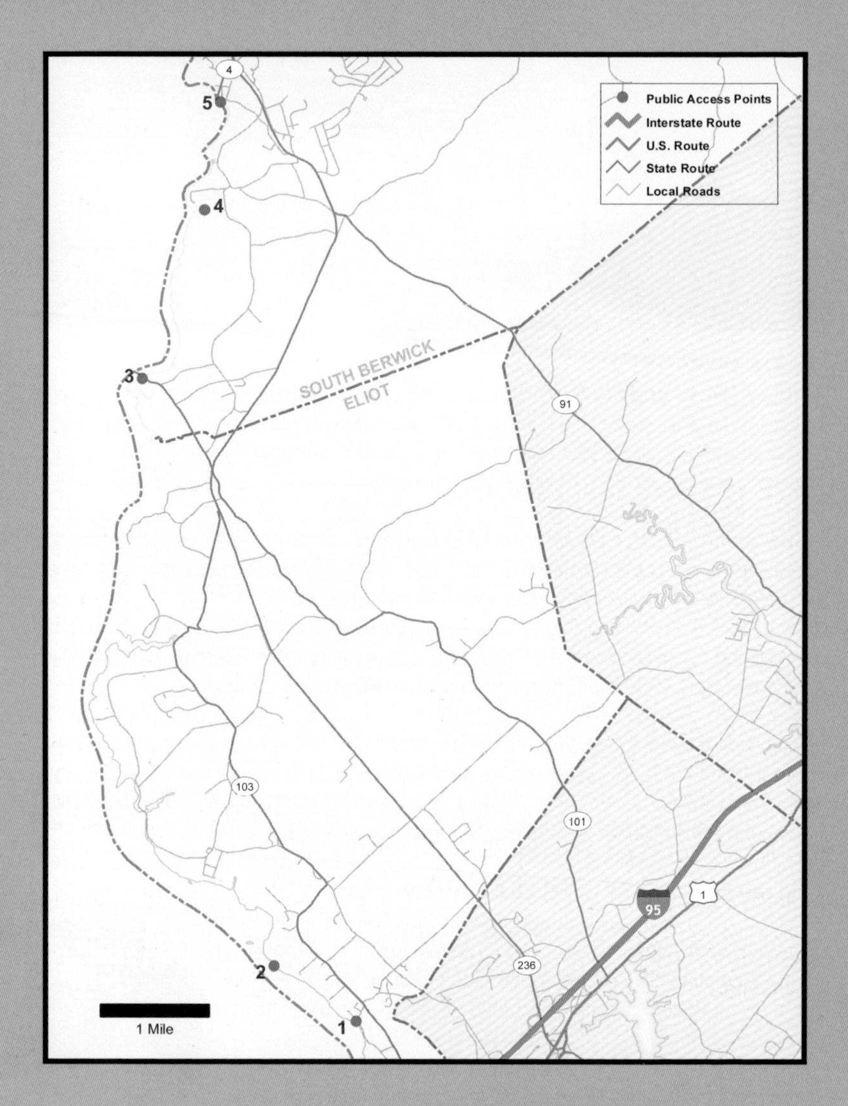

Eliot-South Berwick

1. Pleasant Street Right-of-Way
2. Piscataqua Boat Basin/Dead Duck Landing
3. William A. Bray Memorial Park
4. Vaughan Woods State Park
5. Counting House Park

Eliot-South Berwick

1. Pleasant Street Right-of-Way

A paved path leads from Pleasant Ave to a small rocky area and the Piscataqua River, where a municipal pier was formerly located. People walk their dogs here.

Directions & Parking: From junction of ME 103/Main St and Bolt Hill Rd in South Eliot, go southeast and take the first right onto Pleasant St. The right-of-way begins immediately after Riverside Ave joins from the right. Limited parking is available on-street.
Lat/Long: 43.1041, -70.7819

2. Piscataqua Boat Basin/Dead Duck Landing

This state-owned facility, operated by the Town of Eliot under a lease agreement, has a concrete ramp and floating dock on 9+ acres, providing motored craft with access to the Piscataqua River, Portsmouth Harbor and the Gulf of Maine. In season, the 103-foot ramp is in constant use (fee charged from Memorial Day weekend to Labor Day weekend). Small-boat users may hand-carry and launch from the wading beach next to the ramp, which may also be used for swimming at low tide; swimming is not permitted from the boat ramp or floats. This site also offers extensive land-based activities, including playing fields, a playground, and a picnic area with covered tables and individual grills. A pavilion (accessible) has a larger grill, water supply and electricity; this facility can be reserved for a small fee from May through mid-October. Leashed dogs are allowed. Accessible bathrooms are located near the upper parking lot.

Directions & Parking: Heading northwest on ME 103/Main St from South Eliot, turn left on Hammond Ln (also known as Junkins Ln) and follow to the end. Park trailers in the lower area, which can fill quickly.
Lat/Long: 43.1113, -70.7972

3. William A. Bray Memorial Park

This 3-acre town park on the shore of the Salmon Falls River provides nice views of the undeveloped river and a part-tide gravel boat launch. Fishing enthusiasts enjoy dropping a line from the nearby bridge.

Directions & Parking: From South Berwick, go about 4 miles south on ME 236, then turn right onto ME 101. Go 1.1 miles to the river. Parking is limited; few trailers can be accommodated.
Lat/Long: 43.1896, -70.8239

William A. Bray Memorial Park

Vaughan Woods State Park

4. Vaughan Woods State Park

This 250-acre park features trail loops that can be linked for a 3-mile walk through woods that include stands of old-growth pine and hemlock, and provide vistas of the Salmon Falls River. The area offers opportunities for birding (best in early morning), viewing plants and mammals, and horseback riding. The trails, on gravel or duff, vary from gentle terrain to steep slopes. The picnic area and restrooms are generally accessible. Leashed dogs are allowed; an entrance fee is charged.

Directions & Parking: From South Berwick, go south on ME 236 for about half a mile; opposite the school, turn right onto Vine St. Continue about one mile to the intersection of Vine and Old Fields Rd. Turn right and watch for the park entrance on the right. The park has an off-street lot with about two dozen spaces.
Lat/Long: 43.2120, -70.8124

5. Counting House Park

This inviting park on the Salmon Falls River, which offers a grassy picnic area, benches, and hand-carry launch site, lies at the base of the easternmost of the river's dams. The three tidal miles on the Salmon Falls River are relatively undeveloped, providing an opportunity for lovely, quiet paddling along wooded shores. The four hours centered on high tide are best, as one stretch becomes quite shallow at low tide. (High tide where the Salmon Falls River meets the Cocheco River to form the Piscataqua River runs 1 hour, 35 minutes after high tide in Portland.)

Directions & Parking: From the east, take ME 236 into South Berwick, turn left onto ME 4 and go 0.3 mile; turn left onto Liberty St at the Counting House Museum. The park, with a small dirt lot, is on the right.
Lat/Long: 43.2267, -70.8105

Counting House Park

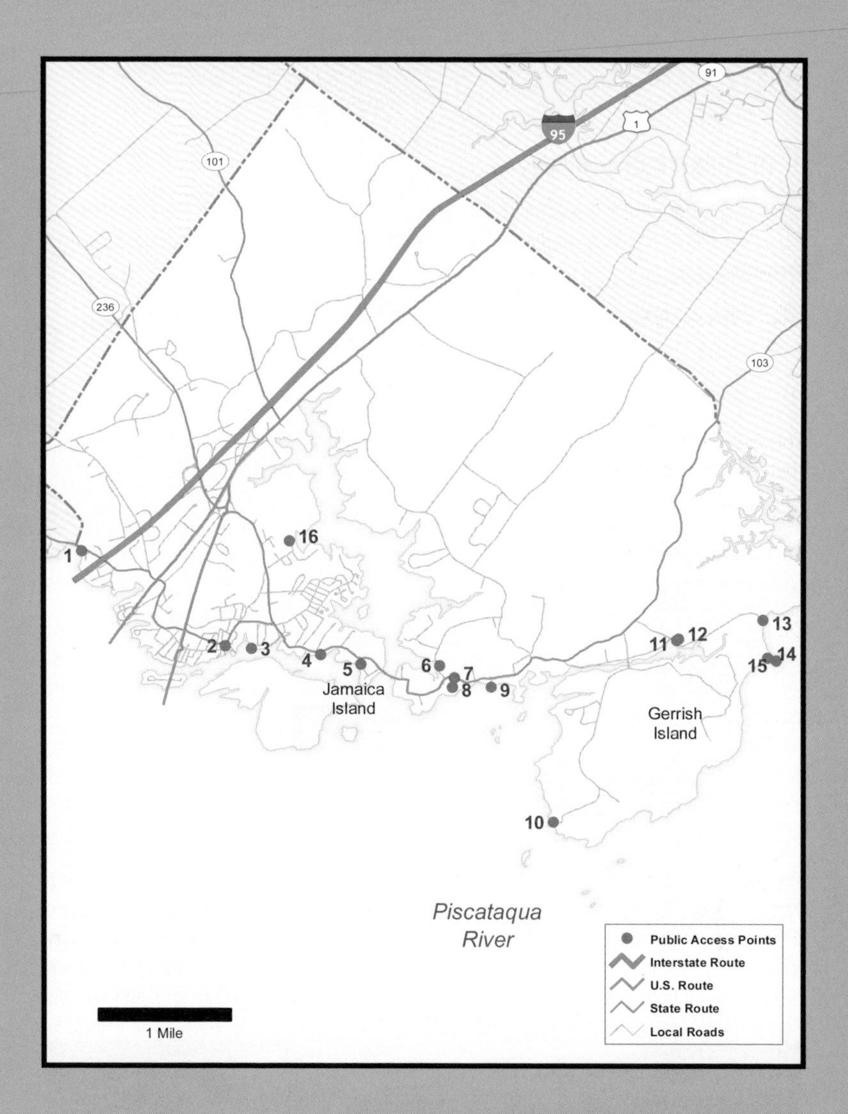

Kittery

1. Old Road Right-of-Way
2. Government Street Town Pier
3. Traip Academy Boat Ramp
4. Whipple Road Right-of-Way
5. Old Ferry Lane Right-of-Way
6. Barter's Creek Right-of-Way
7. Fairchild Conservation Easement
8. Fort McClary State Historic Site
9. Kittery Point Town Pier and Boat Ramp
10. Fort Foster Park
11. Cutts Island Lane Right-of-Way
12. Cutts Island Trail
13. Seapoint Beach
14. Crescent Beach
15. Seapoint
16. Rogers Park

See next page for Kittery Listings ➤

Kittery

1. Old Road Right-of-Way

Located in a residential area, this short path leads to a rocky area/mud flat across from a boatyard and next to a causeway. An old barge lies in the mud. This is not the most scenic area, but it does provide a place for people to fish.

Directions & Parking: Cross Spinney Creek going east on ME 103/South Eliot Rd, take Spinney Cove Dr south, and immediately turn right on a dead end road with limited parking at the end. **Lat/Long:** 43.0960, -70.7650

2. Government Street Town Pier

Commercial fishermen are the primary users of this small public wharf (no float or ramp).

Directions & Parking: The pier is north of Seavey's Island, immediately west of the Walker St bridge. From ME 103/Government St and Route 1, go east 0.4 mile and take a right on Town Wharf Rd to extremely limited parking and many "No Parking" signs.
Lat/Long: 43.0851, -70.7434

3. Traip Academy Boat Ramp

This paved, all-tide boat ramp, which has a dock and small float, provides access to the Piscataqua River for everyone from commercial fishermen to duck hunters, bass fishermen, sea kayakers and others. A fee is charged; season permits are available.

Directions & Parking: The ramp, next to Traip Academy, faces Seavey's Island; it is between the Walker St and Wyman Ave bridges. From ME 103/Whipple Rd between the two bridges, turn south on Williams Ave to the school and continue to the far end of its lot, where there is very limited parking (some of which is designated accessible) at the ramp. When the school is not in use, visitors may park there. **Lat/Long:** 43.0858, -70.7394

Traip Academy Boat Ramp

4. Whipple Road Right-of-Way

This tiny area, formerly the location of a town fishing pier, offers a place to walk to the water or tie up a boat.

Directions & Parking: On ME 103/Whipple Rd east of the Wyman Ave bridge to the shipyard – just after the junction with Tilton Ave – a break in the guard rail opens to the right-of-way path. A grassy path leads to the water. Park tightly against the guard rail.
Lat/Long: 43.0853, -70.7290

5. Old Ferry Lane Right-of-Way

Paddlers can hand-carry and launch into Back Channel opposite Jamaica Island at this part-tide site. A concrete/stone mooring tie-up lies at the water's edge.

Directions & Parking: From the Wyman Ave bridge onto Seavey's Island, go east on ME 103 for 0.7 mile and veer right onto Old Ferry Ln. The right-of-way is immediately on the right, just beyond a small cove and before a house. On-street parking is very limited. An opening in a hedge leads to a mowed area and down to a small stone pier.
Lat/Long: 43.0844, -70.7229

6. Barter's Creek Right-of-Way

A short trail through the woods leads to a tidal inlet with a rock ledge. Anglers can cast here, paddlers can launch a canoe or kayak, and people can swim, but all activities are tide dependent.

Directions & Parking: From Kittery, go east on ME 103/Whipple Rd to the Kittery Point bridge; continue on ME 103/Pepperrell Rd for about a mile, turning left onto Crockett Neck Rd. Park off-road (very limited) on the right immediately before the causeway over Barter's Creek. Access is next to the culvert.
Lat/Long: 43.0844, -70.7110

7. Fairchild Conservation Easement

This 17-acre Kittery Land Trust easement offers a short walk through hardwoods and pines to shoreland overlooking Chauncey Creek.

Directions & Parking: From Ft McClary State Park in Kittery Point, go east on ME 103 for about a mile, veer right on Chauncey Creek Rd, and take the first right onto Gerrish Island Rd. Turn right onto Pocahontas and go 0.2 mile. Look for a brass "8" at a driveway. The driveway itself is private so park on the street. The trail starts a few steps down the drive, on the right. **Lat/Long:** 43.0834, -70.6858

8. Fort McClary State Historic Site

The white hexagonal fort, earthworks, and jumble of granite blocks offer a view into history. In 1808, when this fort was being built, veterans of the Revolutionary War and their families still bore the losses of the conflict. Major Andrew McClary, a New Hampshire native, had died at Bunker Hill; this fort was named in his honor. From the mowed grounds, visitors can look out onto a flotilla of sailboats in Portsmouth Harbor, with two sentinel structures: Portsmouth Harbor Light, located next to Fort Constitution on New Castle Island to the south, and Whaleback Light, to the southwest. Across the street from the fort, there's a picnic area and a shelter.

Directions & Parking: From Kittery, go east on ME 103/Whipple Rd to the Kittery Point bridge. Continue on ME 103/Pepperrell Rd for about half a mile, then turn right at the sign and park in one of two lots. **Lat/Long:** 43.0821, -70.7091

Kittery Point Town Pier

9. Kittery Point Town Pier and Boat Ramp

This very busy site on Portsmouth Harbor has two piers, a floating dock and a part-tide paved boat ramp (fee), all of which are tucked behind Enoteca's Market. Commercial fishermen are regulars, along with those who are shore fishing for mackerel and winter flounder. Temporary docking only is permitted. Bathrooms are located next to ramp.

Directions & Parking: Take ME 103 east to Kittery Point Village. Opposite the Post Office, turn right onto Bellamy Ln, which leads to the water. Parking on-site is mostly restricted or reserved; there is a fee to park in the lot at the top of hill opposite the market. When school is not in session, boaters may park at nearby Mitchell School, which has space for both vehicles and trailers. **Lat/Long:** 43.0821, -70.7033

10. Fort Foster Park

The view from this 94-acre town park at the mouth of the Piscataqua River is stupendous: On a clear day, you can see Whaleback Light, Wood Island Lifeboat Station and the Isles of Shoals. The northernmost section of the park has picnic tables and grills and a sandy/pebbly beach. A long pier juts into the water, providing an extensive platform for fishing. To the southeast, a separate area, with a crescent of sand ideal for launching, has been set aside for windsurfers and sea kayakers. Scuba diving is allowed anywhere outside of the main beach area. A trail runs above the high tide line along the park's shore. Concrete bunkers and fortifications, built in the early 1900s, serve as a universal backdrop. Dogs are allowed in most areas but must be leashed. Park users must carry out their trash. Motorized watercraft, ATVs and dirt bikes are not allowed. The park (fee charged) is open during the summer and weekends at the beginning and end of the season.

Directions & Parking: From Kittery Point, take ME 103 east, veer right on Gerrish Island Rd, turn right on Pocahontas, and follow signs for Ft Foster. Park in one of several lots, depending on activity. **Lat/Long:** 43.0676, -70.6935

11. Cutts Island Lane Right-of-Way

From this boat launch, kayakers and canoeists can head south along Chauncey Creek or – tide level permitting – north into Brave Boat Harbor. The site is located almost opposite the Cutts Island trailhead.

Directions & Parking: Use directions for Cutts Island Trail. Along the causeway on the right, a break in the guard rail allows hand-carry access to a tiny stone ramp.
Lat/Long: 43.0877, -70.6756

12. Cutts Island Trail

This 1.8-mile wooded trail provides upland hiking, lovely views of the salt marsh, and birding opportunities in the Rachel Carson National Wildlife Refuge. The trail is open sunrise to sunset to foot traffic only; pets are not allowed. Hunters with a refuge permit can hunt here, so visitors should wear orange in the fall. A permanent outhouse is located at the trail head which also serves the Cutts Island Lane Right-of-Way carry-in kayak or canoe access site.

Directions & Parking: From Kittery Point Village, take ME 103 east, veer right on Gerrish Island Rd, and go almost a mile to a causeway. The trailhead is on the east end of the causeway, on the left; on-street parking is very limited.
Lat/Long: 43.0879, -70.6754

Seapoint Beach

13. Seapoint Beach

This beach is a quarter-mile crescent of fine sand backed by cobbles and marsh. It's a lovely place to swim, sunbathe, and take in the long view of the rolling Atlantic. There are no bathrooms here, but the nearby Cutts Island Trail has a composting toilet at the trailhead. In summer, dogs are not allowed during the day; the beach and parking area are closed at night.

Directions & Parking: From Kittery Point Village, take ME 103 east, veer right on Gerrish Island Rd, and continue to the causeway when it becomes Seapoint Rd. Go about 0.6 mile; Seapoint Rd goes right, ending at the water. In summer, parking (along the road) is strictly limited to Kittery residents with a landfill sticker.
Lat/Long: 43.0902, -70.6628

14. Crescent Beach

Crescent and Seapoint Beaches flank Seapoint on the northeast corner of Gerrish Island facing the open ocean. Crescent is about a third of a mile, with a bed of small rocks and a bit of sand. On a mild day, the waves lap at the shore; when the wind rises, they roll up the beach, leaving wrack and driftwood in straggling lines. A marsh behind the beach, part of the Rachel Carson National Wildlife Refuge, offers good birding. Composting toilets are located at nearby Cutts Island Trail.

Directions & Parking: Access is from Seapoint Beach.
Lat/Long: 43.0851, -70.6641

Seapoint

15. Seapoint

The Kittery Land Trust owns this rocky 2-acre finger of land that anchors beaches to the north and south. From here, on a clear day, visitors can view Nubble Light, Isles of Shoals and Cape Ann. Given the restrictions on nearby parking, Seapoint (as well as Crescent and Seapoint Beaches) is the perfect destination for bicyclists: Ride out, take in the stupendous scenery, eat a picnic lunch, and head back. Leashed dogs are allowed. Composting toilets are located at nearby Cutts Island Trail.

Directions & Parking: Access is from Seapoint Beach.
Lat/Long: 43.0858, -70.6606

16. Rogers Park

A wide, airy trail through mixed woods leads to salt marsh and, at low tide, mud flats of the west shore of Spruce Creek. Birders enjoy the variety in habitat, with the opportunity to see both land birds and waterbirds on this 27-acre parcel. The occasional bench and picnic table offer opportunities to nibble on a sandwich or watch squirrels scamper through the trees. Clamming is walk-in only. Well-behaved dogs are welcome.

Directions & Parking: From I-95, take the Kittery exit. At the rotary, take ME 236/Rogers Rd, turn left in half a mile onto Dion Ave, bear left at the "T," and go to limited parking at the end of the road.
Lat/Long: 43.0977, -70.7340

Rogers Park

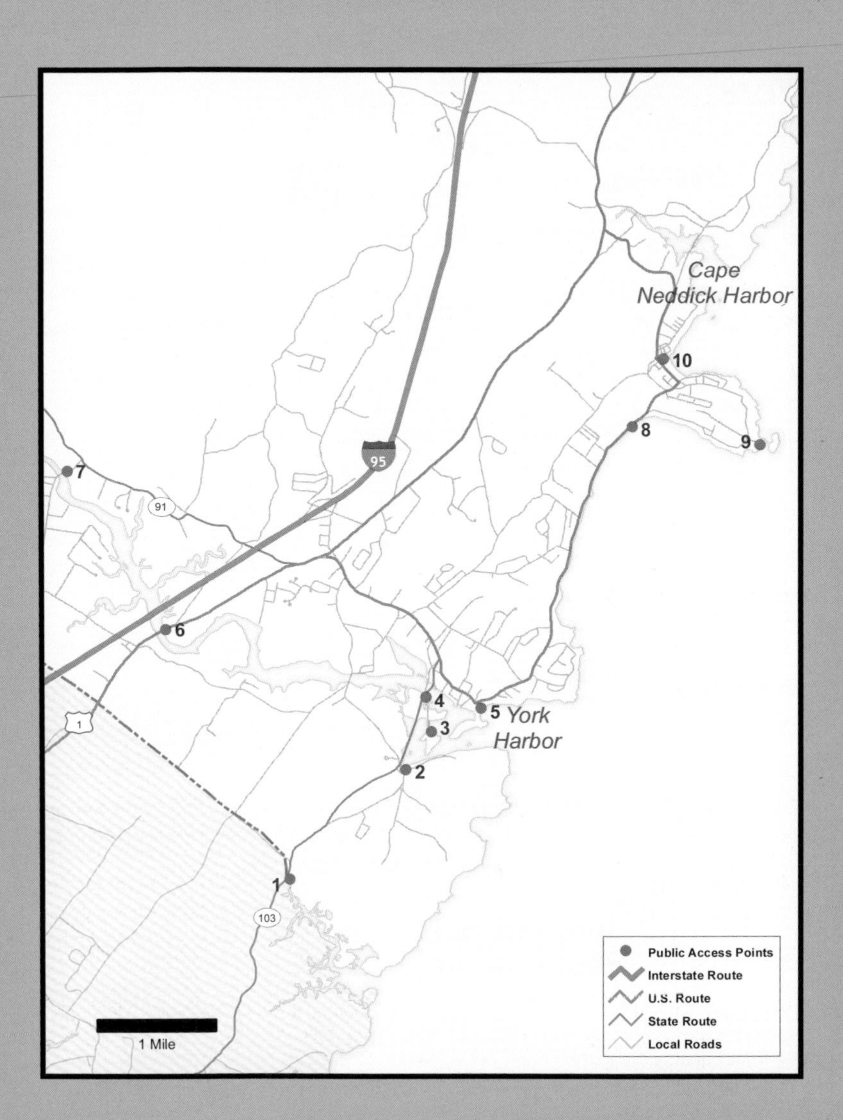

York

1. Brave Boat Tidal Creek Fishing Access
2. Seabury Gut
3. Town Dock #2
4. Strawberry Island Launch
5. Harbor Beach
6. Rice's Bridge
7. Scotland Bridge
8. Long Sands Beach
9. Nubble Light and Sohier Park
10. Short Sands Beach

See next page for York Listings ➤

York

1. Brave Boat Tidal Creek Fishing Access 

This serene, undeveloped stretch of tidal creek offers anglers a chance to cast a line and capture some respite from a busy life. People may fish from dawn to dusk on the north bank, from the bridge to the first trestle downstream – about a 1,000 foot shoreline overall. Because this land is part of the Rachel Carson National Wildlife Refuge, both refuge regulations (use non-lead jigs and sinkers only to prevent waterbird poisoning; attend lines at all times; carry out all litter including monofilament, which can be dangerous to wildlife; collect no bait fish) as well as Maine fishing regulations apply. It is possible to hand-carry and launch a small boat here. User cooperation is important for the site to remain available; visitors should obey refuge rules and respect private property.

Directions & Parking: From York Harbor, go south on ME 103 (runs into Brave Boat Harbor Rd, passes Payne Rd on the right) for about 2 miles. Park on the main road next to the creek between Payne and bridge (space is limited), as there is no parking at the refuge. Walk south to the bridge. **Lat/Long:** 43.1117, -70.6700

2. Seabury Gut 

This short path is used primarily for access to shellfishing. It is possible to hand-carry and launch a boat, but beware of the tide schedule, as this launch has tide-limited access.

Directions & Parking: From the York Harbor bridge, take ME 103 south 0.7 mile, turn left on Seabury Rd and left again on Western Point Rd. Immediately look for a small path to the water on the left. Parking is minimal, on-street. **Lat/Long:** 43.1252, -70.6511

3. Town Dock #2

The southern side of York Harbor offers recreational boaters a fixed dock with floats and a portable toilet. The harbormaster's office is located here; a marina and restaurants can be found nearby. Fishermen may cast a line during daylight hours, but swimming is not permitted.

Directions & Parking: Immediately south of the York Harbor bridge, turn east from ME 103 onto Harris Island Rd, where there are about two dozen spots (but no trailer parking). **Lat/Long:** 43.1298, -70.6471

4. Strawberry Island Launch 

This small, pebbly beach on the southern side of York Harbor provides canoeists and sea kayakers with a launch site that is separate from motored craft; boats with motors may not be launched here during the summer.

Directions & Parking: Follow directions to Town Dock #2, but stop at Strawberry Island, to the left just before the dock and parking area, to drop your boat before you park. **Lat/Long:** 43.1338, -70.6475

Harbor Beach

5. Harbor Beach

At low tide, beach lovers can settle in to a wide area of fine sand; when the tide comes in, there's still room to spread out a towel on this quarter-mile-long beach. Western Point and Black Rocks (shoals to the east) offer protection from the large swells of the open ocean, making this an appealing place to dabble in the water. A lifeguard is on duty during the summer. In addition to offering its own beauty, the beach anchors two scenic walks: Cliff Path follows the northern shore for half a mile, and Fisherman's Walk runs southwest along the north shore of the York River to ME 103. Hartley Mason Park, on the southwest corner of the beach, offers scenic views and an interpretive sign. Boaters may not hand-carry and launch here. Restrooms are available on Harbor Beach Rd.

Directions & Parking: From York Harbor, go east on Route 1A/York St past Stage Neck and turn right on Harbor Beach Rd. On the road and at the beach lot, parking is restricted to town residents with a permit. Public parking (with time restrictions) is available along Route 1A. **Lat/Long:** 43.1328, -70.6388

6. Rice's Bridge 

When the Department of Transportation created this hand-carry launch in the late 1990s as part of its work on Route 1, boaters and fishermen were delighted. The site, located immediately east of Route 1 and I-95, provides all-tide access to the York River, though at high tide passage upstream can be limited by the girders supporting the bridge. Fishermen also congregate on the bridge itself. Goodrich Park, operated by the Town of York, is located on the western side of the bridge.

Directions & Parking: From I-95, take exit 7, go 2 miles south on Route 1 and park parallel to the road on the left just before the bridge or in the lot for Goodrich Park.
Lat/Long: 43.1416, -70.6914

7. Scotland Bridge 

The most notable feature of this part-tide gravel boat launch is that it is the only trailerable launch in York. When the river level is high, upstream access can be limited by the girders supporting the bridge.

Directions & Parking: Take exit 7 from I-95, go south on Route 1 and then right on ME 91 under I-95. Go 1.5 miles to a bridge on the left. Only a few vehicles can squeeze onto the gravel shoulder. **Lat/Long:** 43.1604, -70.7083

8. Long Sands Beach 

At almost 1.5 miles, this beach more than lives up to its name. The fine-grained sand is an invitation to set up a lawn chair and umbrella, play in the water, and watch row after row of waves lap against the shore. Surfers (in designated areas during the summer) and anglers enjoy Long Sands as well. At low tide, there are more square feet of sand; the space available at high tide is limited to a narrow border between the beach and Route 1A. A lifeguard is on duty during the summer. The restroom/bathhouse is located near Oceanside Ave. Group games are not permitted on the beach; dogs are not allowed during the daytime in the summer. Arriving by foot or bike solves the parking problem; visitors in vehicles should plan to arrive early to find a parking spot.

Directions & Parking: From York Harbor, take Route 1A north to the beach on the right. There is metered parking along Route 1A; those with a beach pass do not have to feed the meter. **Lat/Long:** 43.1671, -70.6146

9. Nubble Light and Sohier Park

A light keeper's house and a white tower with a black turret stand at the crest of this tiny island just offshore of Cape Neddick. Visitors can take in this classic view of Cape Neddick Light Station from Sohier Park, three acres on the tip of The Nubble, as the peninsula is also called. The bedrock here is gabbro, a dark igneous rock that resists weathering and thus provides endless opportunity for scrambling along the shore. Scuba divers (allowed all days except Sunday) find the area's fish, plant life and steep underwater walls inviting despite slippery entry/exit rocks at low tide. In winter, birders expect the usual ducks and waterbirds, but also scout for unusual species that occasionally fly into view; in the fall, this is a good spot for migrating warblers and sparrows. Other outdoor enthusiasts get out their poles for shore fishing. A seasonal welcome center with gift shop and restrooms are located on-site.

Directions & Parking: From either York or Ogunquit, take Route 1A to Cape Neddick, turning east on Nubble Rd. Parking is free but limited to 2 hours; the two lots fill quickly. **Lat/Long:** 43.1652, -70.5932

10. Short Sands Beach

This hugely popular area might have been designed for beach lovers, for it has more sand at high tide than any of the town's other beaches. Changing rooms, bathrooms, an outdoor shower and seasonal lifeguards are added benefits. Although the beach becomes thick with umbrellas and sunbathers, fishermen do cast from the sand as well. Group games are not permitted; neither surfing nor dogs are allowed during the daytime in the summer. Ellis Park, at the southern end of the beach, provides a picnic area, rest rooms, playground and pavilion. A general store, restaurants, and shops are located nearby.

Directions & Parking: The beach runs between Route 1A/Ocean Ave and the ocean immediately north of Cape Neddick. There is a large metered town lot next to the beach; it fills quickly on hot summer days.
Lat/Long: 43.1755, -70.6095

To Weather a Year on the Beach

Those who frequent Maine's beaches in winter know them not for warm sand and inviting water, but as a place to walk, think and "get away from it all." In winter, the average surface sea temperature hovers between 33 and 36 degrees F. The prevailing winds blow chiefly from the northwest. The damaging storms sweep in from the northeast, stripping the beach of sand and moving it offshore. A storm surge coupled with a high tide can tear out dunes and scatter seaweed, driftwood and debris along the shore.

During the winter months, the action is all off-shore, where a dozen or so hearty species of birds may hang out: loons (common and red-throated), common eider, long-tailed ducks, scoters (black, surf, white-winged), common goldeneye, bufflehead, red-breasted merganser, and grebes (horned and red-necked). Purple sandpipers scurry among the rocks along the edge of the water on a dropping tide. Resident herring and great black-backed gulls cruise over the water, surveying all activity.

In April, things start to change. The water temperature rises to about 40 degrees, barely colder than the air. The prevailing wind shifts into the west or southwest. Less intense storms with more moderate waves begin moving sand from the offshore bar back onto the beach. Greater yellowlegs are common, sometimes abundant as they feed and fatten for the remaining flight north to the tundra. Semipalmated plover, ruddy turnstone, sanderling, semipalmated sandpiper and least sandpiper follow in May, along with other less common species. By June the crowds have moved through.

Annuals like beach pea, sea-kale, saltwort, sea-beach sandwort, sea milkwort, and white sea-blite – plants that have adapted to salt spray and drying wind – grow along the upper berm above wave action. In the dunes, beach grass dominates with (perhaps) small pitch pines or at least pockets of gooseberry, raspberry, beach heather and hearty annuals. The wind is mostly from the southwest. In June, the water averages 53 degrees, the air is in the 60s. Beach-goers hope for warm weekends, more for strolling than wading.

By July and August – high summer - shorebirds return. They have raised their young and are foraging to fuel the balance of their migration south. With water temperatures peaking between 60 and 70 degrees, beach peas are flowering; their seed pods look like pea pods from the garden.

By September and early October the shorebirds are moving on, as have most human visitors. Water temperature has dropped to the low 50s. By November, the loons, sea ducks and other water birds have moved back, riding the waves just offshore. The wind shifts to the northwest. The year has come full circle.

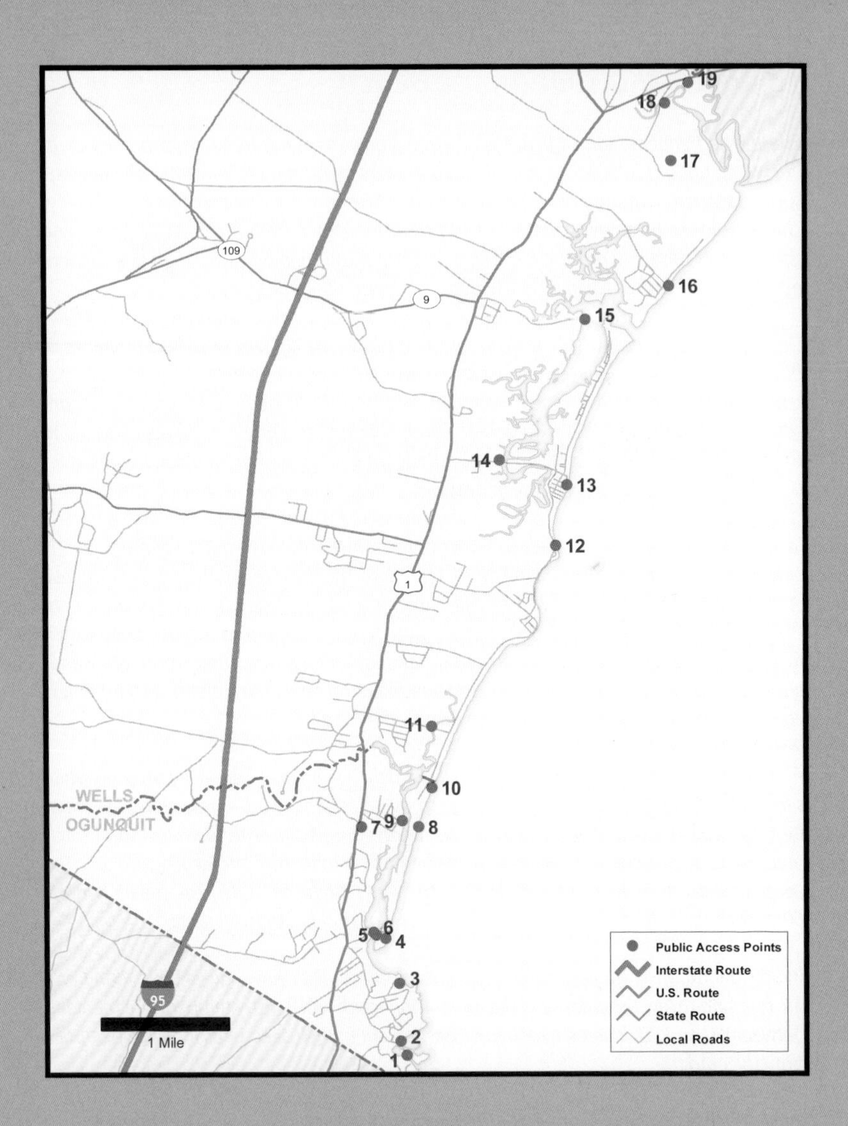

Wells-Ogunquit

1. Perkins Cove Harbor
2. Marginal Way
3. Little Beach
4. Main Beach
5. Riverside Beach
6. Beach Street Bridge
7. Beach Plum Farm Easement
8. Footbridge Beach
9. Footbridge Boat Ramp
10. North Beach
11. Stevens Brook Fishing Access
12. Crescent Beach
13. Wells Beach
14. Webhannet River Fishing Access
15. Webhannet River Boat Launch and Town Landing
16. Drakes Island Beach
17. The Wells National Estuarine Research Reserve – which includes historic Laudholm Farm – offers numerous programs on coasts and estuaries.
18. Merriland River/Skinner Mill Fishing Access
19. Carson Trail

Wells-Ogunquit

Perkins Cove Harbor

1. Perkins Cove Harbor

Perkins Cove is a fishing village transformed into a tourist destination with plenty of restaurants, shops, yachts, cruise boats, and fishing charter boats. It has excellent harbor views and even a manually operated pedestrian footbridge. The busy port has a public dock (docking fees apply) and restrooms. Marginal Way starts here and runs north.

Directions & Parking: From the junction of Route 1 and Ocean Ave, go south on Route 1 for a mile and veer left on Shore Rd. Go almost a mile and turn left on Perkins Cove Rd. Continue halfway down the peninsula to a municipal (fee) lot and 2-hour metered parking spots on the left. **Lat/Long:** 43.2365, -70.5900

2. Marginal Way 

This mile-long, paved coastal footpath – extending from Perkins Cove Harbor to Beach Street in Ogunquit – snakes along the rocky shore between stately homes and the ocean, offering an unparalleled vantage point for viewing the sparkling white sands of Ogunquit and the open ocean. Little Beach, with its enticing slice of sand, lies along the way. Between Memorial Day and Columbus Day, Marginal Way is a major attraction; visitors who want a quiet stroll go very early or off-season.
Directions & Parking: Access is from Perkins Cove, Beach St in Ogunquit or along the way.
Lat/Long: 43.3515, -70.5911

3. Little Beach

This quarter-mile stretch of sand and cobbles lures visitors who are willing to trade vast quantities of sand for more personal space. From here, in the shelter of Israels Head, viewers can take in the Atlantic and the line of beaches to the north. Lifeguards are on duty mid-June through Labor Day. Dogs are not allowed April 1 through September 30. At other times of the year, they must be leashed. The beach is closed at night; camping, fires, fireworks, and smoking are prohibited.

Directions & Parking: From the junction of Route 1/Main St and Ocean Ave, go south on Route 1 for about a mile and veer left on Shore Rd. Go half a mile, turn left on Stearns Rd and look for on-street parking. A set of stairs leads down to the beach. Or, gain access from Marginal Way. **Lat/Long:** 43.2445, -70.5907

4. Main Beach

In summer, sunbathers, body surfers, and surf fishermen line this long, ample sand beach. Visitors through the seasons, however, should be prepared for a changed landscape. In the summer, North and Main Beaches are wide and smooth. In winter, strong waves transfer sand offshore, leaving the berm much narrower. By the next summer, sand has been restored. Lifeguards are on duty mid-June through Labor Day. Dogs are not allowed April 1 through September 30. At other times of the year, they must be leashed. The beach is closed at night; camping, fires, fireworks, and smoking are prohibited. Restrooms are located at the parking lot.

Directions & Parking: From the junction of Route 1/Main St and Ocean Ave, go south on Route 1 for about a mile and turn left on Beach St. A large (fee) parking lot lies at the east end of the bridge next to a hotel complex. **Lat/Long:** 43.2497, -70.5936

5. Riverside Beach

This beach, on the west side of the peninsula, faces the Ogunquit River making it more sheltered from wind and waves than Main or North Beaches. Favorite activities are sunbathing, wading and fishing. Lifeguards are on duty mid-June through Labor Day. Dogs are not allowed April 1 through September 30. At other times of the year, they must be leashed. The beach is closed at night; camping, fires, fireworks, and smoking are prohibited.

Directions & Parking: From the junction of Route 1/Main St and Ocean Ave, go south on Route 1 for about a mile and turn left on Beach St. A large (fee) parking lot lies at the east end of the bridge next to a hotel complex. **Lat/Long:** 43.2500, -70.5951

6. Beach Street Bridge

This bridge connects the mainland with the narrow peninsula of beaches to the east, but it's more than a conduit. There are usually fishermen here, and they congregate when the stripers are running. Although crabbing is not generally considered a popular recreational activity in Maine, this is the perfect spot to do it: Just drop a net bag and see what scuttles in.

Directions & Parking: From the junction of Route 1/Main St and Ocean Ave, go south on Route 1 for about a mile and turn left on Beach St. A large (fee) parking lot lies at the east end of the bridge next to a hotel complex.
Lat/Long: 43.2503, -70.5955

7. Beach Plum Farm Easement

A stone's throw from Route 1, this 22-acre remnant of a saltwater farm offers a glimpse of what life was like a hundred years ago. A footpath traverses upland field, salt marsh and shrubby riparian habitat, encircling more than four dozen community garden plots; a stroll usually takes half an hour, but birders may require longer as it's often a productive area. Great Works Regional Land Trust, which owns the property, is headquartered in one of the barns. The area is open dawn to dusk; pets not allowed; visitors must carry out litter and stay on trails. A portable toilet is stationed at the parking lot.

Directions & Parking: From the center of Ogunquit village, go 0.6 mile north on Route 1. Turn in on Beach Plum Farm Rd (across from Captain Thomas Rd). Park in a very limited lot at the farm entrance. **Lat/Long:** 43.2623, -70.5977

8. Footbridge Beach

This undeveloped beach, which lies between North and Main Beaches, gets its name from the pedestrian bridge over the Ogunquit River that users must cross to gain access to the ocean. Rugosa rose – with its large five-petaled rose-purple flowers –and spiky dune grass line the back shore; a snow fence surrounds and protects the dunes. The view stretches to Israels Head in the distance. Dogs are not allowed April 1 through September 30. At other times of the year, they must be leashed. The beach is closed at night; camping, fires, fireworks, and smoking are prohibited.

Directions & Parking: From Route 1, go east on Ocean Rd to its terminus at a large (fee) lot. Walk across the bridge to the beach. **Lat/Long:** 43.2624, -70.5889

9. Footbridge Boat Ramp

This paved ramp, suitable for launching small boats only, provides access to the Ogunquit River, but the site has physical limits. The ramp is on the north – upstream – side of a low-slung bridge. At high tide, passage downstream beneath the bridge is restricted; at low tide, the ramp is unusable. The bridge itself is a popular fishing site. Great Works Regional Land Trust owns and has conserved a small parcel of salt marsh and uplands next to the parking lot. A restroom is located within easy walking distance.

Directions & Parking: From Route 1, go east on Ocean Rd to its terminus at a large (fee) town lot. **Lat/Long**: 43.2631, -70.5913

10. North Beach

North Beach is the undeveloped stretch that lies between private Moody Beach (cottages to the north) and Footbridge Beach to the south. It is possible to hand-carry a kayak across the road and along a narrow path to launch – surf permitting – at the beach. Dogs are not allowed April 1 through September 30. At other times of the year, they must be leashed. The beach is closed at night; camping, fires, fireworks, and smoking are prohibited.

Directions & Parking: From Ogunquit, go north on Route 1 to Bourne Ave in Wells, turn right on Ocean Ave, and continue to the large (fee) parking lot immediately north of the sewage treatment plant. **Lat/Long:** 43.2669, -70.5868

North Beach

Stevens Brook Fishing Access

11. Stevens Brook Fishing Access

Stevens Brook originates behind Moody Point and snakes south behind the beach to join the Ogunquit River south of Bourne Ave. Fishing is permitted on the east shore about a quarter of a mile from Bourne Ave to the point at which the brook loops next to Ocean Ave. This site lies within the boundaries of the Rachel Carson National Wildlife Refuge. Both refuge regulations (use non-lead jigs and sinkers only to prevent waterbird poisoning; attend lines at all times; carry out all litter including monofilament, which can be dangerous to wildlife; collect no bait fish) as well as Maine fishing regulations apply. User cooperation is important for the site to remain available; visitors should obey refuge rules and respect private property.

Directions & Parking: From the center of Wells, go 3.5 miles south on Route 1, turn left on Bourne Ave, and at the "T" turn right on Ocean Ave. Continue past houses to the public parking lot. **Lat/Long:** 43.2738, -70.5869

12. Crescent Beach

This half-mile area offers some tide pools and rocks as well as a nice stretch of sand for sunbathing. With a spotting scope or hefty binoculars, visitors can watch for seals on Bucklin Rock. Lifeguards are on duty in summer; the beach is closed at night. Dogs are not allowed during the day in summer; at other times, they must be leashed. Portable toilets are located at the parking area.

Directions & Parking: Directions & Parking: From the center of Wells, go 1.3 miles south on Route 1 and turn left on Mile Rd, then right on Webhannet Dr. The beach lies east of the point at which Webhannet and Gold Ribbon Dr join. A lot lies between the two roads; a parking fee is charged at the Gold Ribbon Dr lot. **Lat/Long:** 43.2947, -70.5680

13. Wells Beach

This mile-long beach and the homes that line the backshore are part of a peninsula that stretches north, with the Webhannet River behind it. At low tide the wide, flat beach offers lots of space for sand castles and lawn chairs; lifeguards are on duty during the summer. A rock jetty and parking lot at the mouth of the harbor extend far into the water, forming the beach's northern boundary. Fishermen venture out onto the jetty to try their luck. Shops, restaurants and lodging are nearby. Restrooms are located at the parking lot; the beach is closed at night; dogs are not allowed on the beach during the summer, and at other times they must be leashed.

Directions & Parking: From the center of Wells, go 1.3 miles south on Route 1 and turn left on Mile Rd. There are two parking lots. The first (large, free) is located where Mile Rd joins Atlantic Ave. The second (larger, fee) is located at the north end of Mile Rd.
Lat/Long: 43.3015, -70.5664

14. Webhannet River Fishing Access

Fishing is permitted on the west shore of the Webhannet River, from Mile Rd north to the first tidal creek (about 400 feet). This site lies within the boundaries of the Rachel Carson National Wildlife Refuge. Both refuge regulations (use non-lead jigs and sinkers only to prevent waterbird poisoning; attend lines at all times; carry out all litter including monofilament, which can be dangerous to wildlife; collect no bait fish) as well as Maine fishing regulations apply. User cooperation is important for the site to remain available; visitors should obey refuge rules and respect private property.

Directions & Parking: From the center of Wells, go 1.3 miles south on Route 1 and turn left on Mile Rd. Go about half a mile; the fishing area is on the left bank of the river.
Lat/Long: 43.3042, -70.5768

15. Webhannet River Boat Launch and Town Landing

This part-tide, paved ramp that lies next to a floating dock provides access to the harbor and the open waters of the Gulf of Maine. Both commercial fishing boats and recreational boats moor in the harbor. A marina and restaurant are within walking distance. Fishing is permitted from the town dock. A gazebo and benches are located in a field on the other side of Harbor Rd; there's room to stroll along the sandy shore of the harbor and double back through open land between the road and the tidal inlet to the south. Restrooms are located at the parking lot.

Directions & Parking: From Route 1 in the center of Wells, take Harbor Rd (opposite ME 9/ ME 109) east to its end at a free town lot. Back trailers onto grass.
Lat/Long: 43.3203, -70.5640

16. Drakes Island Beach

This beach joins Laudholm Beach to the north to offer more than half a mile of sand, dunes and ocean. Anglers can fish from the rock jetty next to the parking lot; swimmers, body boarders, skim boarders, and surf kayakers can play in the waves; and everyone can enjoy the lovely fine sand. Lifeguards are on duty in summer; bathrooms are located at the parking lot.

Directions & Parking: From Route 1 in the center of Wells, go a little more than a mile north and turn right on Drakes Island Rd. Park in the town lot on the left as you head toward the water, or take a right on Island Beach Rd and follow it to Foster Ln, where there is another lot; seasonal fees are charged in both places. Follow a path to the beach.
Lat/Long: 43.3244, -70.5510

Drakes Island Beach

17. Wells National Estuarine Research Reserve at Laudholm

The Wells Reserve provides almost a dozen trail loops, adding up to 7 miles that range through fields, woodlands, salt marsh, and beach. Two offer self-guided instruction in ecology: The Salt Marsh Loop shows how precipitation moves through a watershed into an estuary, and the Forest Interpretive Trail looks at how cleared land becomes forest over time, and how that change affects plants and animals. A trail to Laudholm Beach (part of the reserve) allows visitors to enjoy an undeveloped beach, dunes, intertidal areas, and shorebirds. The reserve offers extensive educational programs for children and adults and a visitor center with a gift shop and exhibits. The reserve is open 7 a.m. to sunset, year-round, for walking, wildlife-watching, snowshoeing and cross-country skiing. Smoking, pets and collection of flora or fauna are not allowed; visitors must remain on the trails. There is a seasonal entrance fee.

Directions & Parking: From the center of Wells, at the intersection of ME 109 and Route 1, go north on Route 1/ME 9 for about 1.5 miles and turn right on Laudholm Farm Rd. Follow the signs for less than a mile to the public parking lot. **Lat/Long:** 43.3386, -70.5510

18. Merriland River/Skinner Mill Fishing Access

This site provides access to the Merriland River, which originates in the town of Sanford and slows to a meander as it nears the coast. Anglers may fish from the boundary of the Rachel Carson National Wildlife Refuge downstream – east – for about a thousand feet; the oxbow is included. Both refuge regulations (use non-lead jigs and sinkers only to prevent waterbird poisoning; attend lines at all times; carry out all litter including monofilament, which can be dangerous to wildlife; collect no bait fish) as well as Maine fishing regulations apply. User cooperation is important for the site to remain available; visitors should obey refuge rules and respect private property.

Directions & Parking: From the center of Wells, take Route 1/ME 9 north for two miles, veer right on ME 9, go half a mile, and then take a sharp right on Skinner Mill Rd. Cross the bridge to the south shore. There is no dedicated refuge parking; park on the shoulder. Take a trail, which runs across private property, to the fishing area. **Lat/Long:** 43.3451, -70.5524

19. Carson Trail

The headquarters of the Rachel Carson National Wildlife Refuge is located here. The one-mile, wheelchair accessible trail, bordered on the east by the Little River, winds through a white pine forest that opens on the south to an expanse of salt marsh, with beach and ocean views beyond. Visitors can use a brochure to guide themselves to a dozen stations. Wading birds, various species of nesting sparrows, and migrating waterfowl and shorebirds can be seen in season. Visitors are asked to stay on the trail to protect fragile vegetation. The trail is open dawn to dusk; the site has a composting toilet; and leashed dogs are allowed. Local knowledge: Salt marsh mosquitoes may be plentiful in the summer.

Directions & Parking: From the junction of Route 1 and ME 9 in Wells, go almost one mile east on ME 9; look for a brown wooden sign on the right and turn in to a parking lot with limited spaces next to the road. **Lat/Long:** 43.3475, -70.5484

Wells National Estuarine Research Reserve

The Wells National Estuarine Research Reserve at Laudholm is a national treasure: A former saltwater farm with 2,250 acres of protected land, whose buildings have been renovated to serve 21st-century science-based activities. The organization's mission is to advance knowledge and stewardship of coasts and estuaries through science, education and conservation.

The reserve serves as a living laboratory for scientists who want to learn about coastal ecosystems and the human role in shaping and caring for the landscape. Areas of study include fish food webs and habitat value, land use impacts on watersheds, salt marsh response to land use and climate change, and biological productivity of estuaries. Researchers continually monitor trends in weather, water quality, nutrients, and plant and animal communities.

The grounds are open to the public every day, providing visitors with the opportunity to use miles of trails that wind through fields, woods, and along the shore. A Visitors' Center offers exhibits and activities. Through a range of programs, educators reach more than 3,000 students and adults annually and provide resource managers, regulators, policymakers and other decision-makers with information on sound coastal management.

Reserve staff members actively manage about 500 upland acres for a range of flora and fauna, serving as a model for stewardship and providing technical assistance, conservation data and other information to communities and organizations to help them conserve their own natural resources.

The reserve is supported through a partnership between Laudholm Trust, a Maine non-profit, and the National Oceanic and Atmospheric Administration. It is one of 28 reserves from Alaska to Puerto Rico.

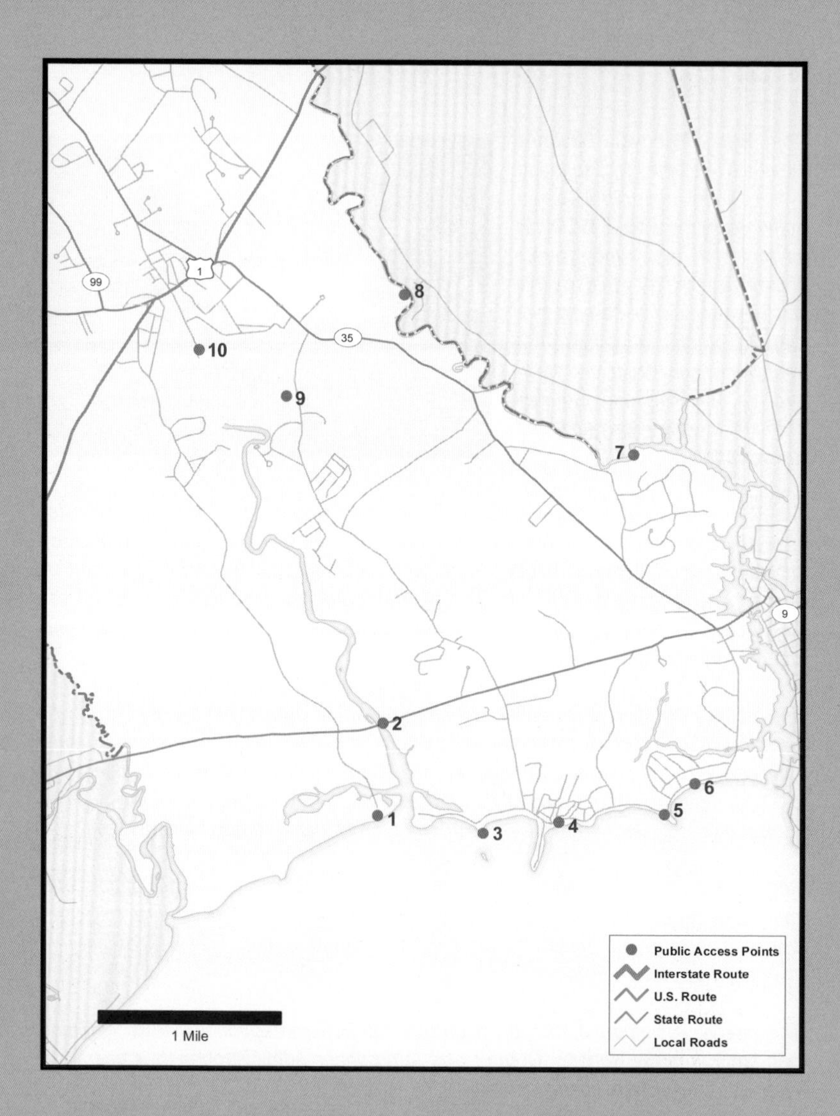

Kennebunk

1. Parsons Beach
2. Mousam River Fishing Access
3. Strawberry Island Preserve
4. Mother's Beach
5. Middle Beach
6. Gooch's Beach/Kennebunk Beach
7. Butler Preserve
8. Wonder Brook Park and Wonder Brook Preserve
9. Sea Road Preserve
10. Mousam River Wildlife Sanctuary

Kennebunk

1. Parsons Beach 

Public use is limited to the northeast end of this lovely beach, located at the mouth of the Mousam River where it wraps around a marsh. The area is ideal for walking, swimming, birding, and simply enjoying the sand. Striper fishermen also value the opportunity to cast for their favorite species. Wild roses and beach grass cover the dunes, providing an attractive backdrop. Limited parking makes it an ideal biking destination. A private family graciously provides access to this beach; public cooperation is paramount. Collection of animal, marine or plant life; walking through the dunes; camping; fires; private parties; surfboards/surfing or use of motorized vehicles are all prohibited. From late spring to early fall, dogs are allowed only on the east end of the beach.

Directions & Parking: From Route 1/Main St in Kennebunk, turn onto Summer St/ME 35 and go 0.6 mile. Turn right onto Sea Rd and go 2.4 miles. Turn right onto ME 9 /Western Ave and go 0.9 mile, then turn left onto Parsons Beach Rd and continue to the end. Parking (parallel, along the road) is very limited past the bridge. Follow the path to the beach. **Lat/Long:** 43.3443, -70.5181

2. Mousam River Fishing Access

People can fish within the Rachel Carson National Wildlife Refuge from the Bridle Path that leads south from ME 9. Fishing is permitted along a 0.3-mile section east of ME 9, on the north side of the river, west to the posted boundary and east to the point opposite Great Hill Road. Access is from the bridle path along the first tidal creek; the trail itself leads onto the Kennebunk Land Trust's Marx Preserve. Fishing is also allowed on the opposite bank and at the mouth of the Mousam River. Both refuge regulations (use non-lead jigs and sinkers only to prevent waterbird poisoning; attend lines at all times; carry out all litter including monofilament, which can be dangerous to wildlife; collect no bait fish) as well as Maine fishing regulations apply. User cooperation is important for the site to remain available; visitors should obey refuge rules and respect private property.

Directions & Parking: From Route 1/Main St in Kennebunk, go southeast on ME 35/ Summer St for 0.6 mile. Turn right on Sea Rd and follow for 2.4 miles. Turn right onto ME 9/ Western Ave and go 0.6 mile to limited parking along the road. The trail is located opposite the pump station. **Lat/Long:** 43.3518, -70.5164

3. Strawberry Island Preserve

This quiet Kennebunk Land Trust property abuts Libby Cove Beach. A narrow path with a bench leads through brush and beach rose to a scenic, rocky shore and a peninsula with a sandbar, ideal for low tide exploration. The amount of dry land, sandbar and water varies with the tide.

Directions & Parking: From Route 1/Main St in Kennebunk, turn onto Summer St/ME 35 and go 0.6 mile. Turn right onto Sea Rd and go about 3 miles to the intersection with Great Hill Rd/Beach Ave. Turn right onto Great Hill Rd and proceed about 0.25 mile to the preserve on the left, with a land trust sign marking the entrance. There is minimal parking on the shoulder; there is also parking along Great Hill Rd.
Lat/Long: 43.3435, -70.5067

4. Mother's Beach 

This 750-foot beach, tucked into a sandy cove adjacent to a residential area, is sheltered and well protected. A popular family choice, the site includes tide pools with crabs and miniature sea creatures, gentle waves and a playground. Seasonal lifeguards are on duty, but there are no facilities. In summer no pets are allowed on the beach and in the off season, dogs must be leashed.

Directions & Parking: From Kennebunk travel southeast on ME 9A/ME 35/Summer St for 0.6 mile. Turn right onto Sea Rd and go 3.1 miles to the end. Turn left onto Beach Ave and go 0.2 mile to limited on-street parking (town permit needed) and the beach.
Lat/Long: 43.3440, -70.4990

5. Middle Beach 

This quarter-mile beach sings at high tide: When waves splash over the bank of small black rocks, the trickling water jostles the pebbles, making them click and hum a soft song. In addition to the acoustics, this area offers an expansive view of the Gulf of Maine, good opportunities for children (or adults) to explore tide pools, and scuba access to the depths. Low tide reveals patches of sand for those who need to fill their quota for barefoot time.

Directions & Parking: From Kennebunk travel south on ME 9A/ME 35/Summer St for 0.6 mile. Turn right onto Kennebunk Beach Rd/Sea Rd and go 3.1 miles to the end. Turn left on Beach Ave and go 0.6 mile to shoulder parking (town permit needed) and the beach on the right. **Lat/Long:** 43.3447, -70.4868

6. Gooch's Beach/Kennebunk Beach

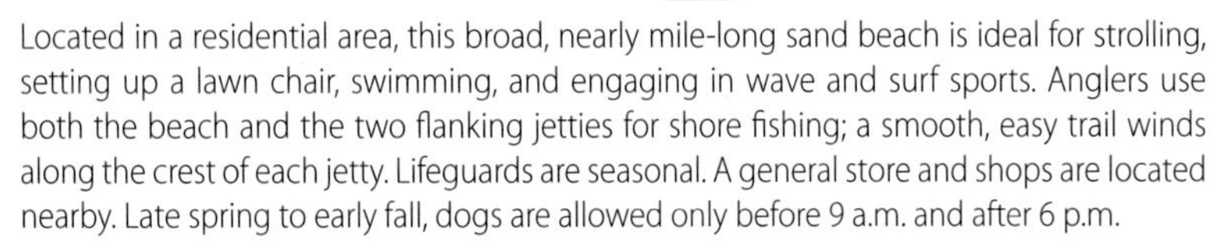

Located in a residential area, this broad, nearly mile-long sand beach is ideal for strolling, setting up a lawn chair, swimming, and engaging in wave and surf sports. Anglers use both the beach and the two flanking jetties for shore fishing; a smooth, easy trail winds along the crest of each jetty. Lifeguards are seasonal. A general store and shops are located nearby. Late spring to early fall, dogs are allowed only before 9 a.m. and after 6 p.m.

Directions & Parking: From Kennebunk go south on ME 9A/ME 35/Summer St for 3.5 miles. At the intersection of ME 9/Western Ave continue straight onto Beach Ave. There is on-street parking; a permit is required. **Lat/Long:** 43.3473, -70.4833

7. Butler Preserve

This 14-acre Kennebunk Land Trust area, also known as Picnic Rock, is a quiet, densely forested preserve situated along a bend in the still-tidal Kennebunk River. It's a lovely spot for a picnic and swimming. A 2-mile scenic woodland trail leads to a ledge overlook (the namesake rock) that provides views up and down the river. The wide, flat path leads through mixed conifers – red pine, white pine, spruce, hemlock and balsam fir – with native wildflowers sprinkled throughout. Some visitors swim; others picnic; others look for native wild flowers in the spring; and still others carry binoculars (cormorants dally on the water and sandpipers scurry along the shore). Regardless of activity, visitors should beware of poison ivy. Open during daylight hours, the preserve has no facilities; fires, camping and motorized vehicles are prohibited.

Directions & Parking: From Kennebunk go southeast on ME 9A/ME 35/Summer St for 2 miles. Take a slight left onto Old Port Rd, travel 0.7 mile to a turnout on the left before River's Edge Dr. Park along Old Port Rd (limited shoulder parking) and walk along the woods road/path to a loop that leads to Picnic Rock, a large glacial boulder. **Lat/Long:** 43.3709, -70.4933

8. Wonder Brook Park and Wonder Brook Preserve

These sites, managed by the Town of Kennebunk and the Kennebunk Land Trust, offer a wooded, 3-mile hike close to the center of town with views of Wonder Brook and the Kennebunk River. There's no map at the trailhead, but the trails are well-marked. Small brooks gurgle as the trail ends near but not at the river. The hike offers vibrant songbirds in the spring and views of wading birds in the river in summer; at dusk, bats dive for insects. Picnic tables are located at the parking area.

Directions & Parking: From Route 1/Main St in Kennebunk, turn southeast onto Summer St. Follow for 0.6 mile and turn left onto Plummer St, going to the small parking lot and trail access at the end. **Lat/Long:** 43.3849, -70.5249

9. Sea Road Preserve

Three public properties – the Bridle Path, owned by the Town of Kennebunk; Sea Road Preserve, owned by the Kennebunk Land Trust; and Rachel Carson National Wildlife Refuge – offer visitors a quiet and protected natural area just a few miles from busy downtown Kennebunk. The Bridle Path runs along an old trolley bed, providing an easy grade that is perfect for strolling, biking, skiing or snowshoeing. Visitors can take the path for a short distance to gain access to trails within the 13-acre preserve. These trails through mixed woods offer scenic views of the tidal Mousam River; several side trails lead steeply down to the water.

Directions & Parking: From Route 1 in Kennebunk, go north and take a right on ME 9A/ ME 35/Summer St. Go half a mile and turn right on Sea Rd. Turn right at the sign for Sea Rd School. Park on a wide dirt pull-off located just before the school's parking lot.
Lat/Long: 43.3773, 70.5288

10. Mousam River Wildlife Sanctuary

This 38-acre Kennebunk Land Trust preserve offers an exceptional view of the estuary along a pair of trails with a combined length of 1.5 miles. The trails lead through dense woods punctuated with benches and scenic overlooks of the serene, meandering river; the site protects more than 2,400 feet of river frontage. The preserve is open during daylight hours; fires, camping and motorized vehicles are prohibited; there are no facilities, but there are picnic tables at Rogers Park, a short distance away.

Directions & Parking: From Main St/Route 1 in Kennebunk, turn onto Water St; continue to the sign, with very limited parking on the left. (There is additional parking at Rogers Pond on Water St.) Walk to the end of the road to a kiosk, which has a map, and the trailhead. **Lat/Long:** 43.3808, -70.5387

Mousam River Wildlife Sanctuary

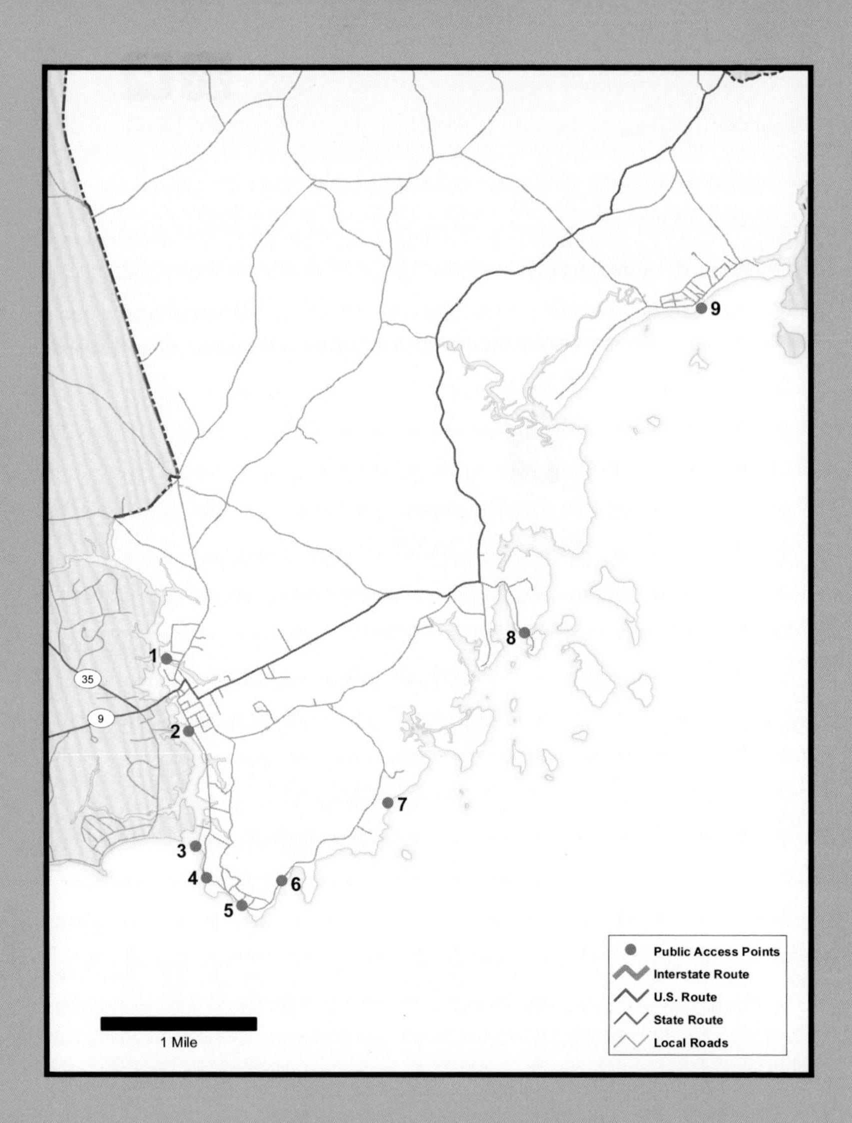

Kennebunkport

1. Grist Mill Property
2. Silas Perkins Park
3. Breakwater/Colony Beach
4. Parsons Way
5. Spouting Rock
6. Blowing Cave
7. Cleaves Cove Beach
8. Causeway Launching Area
9. Goose Rocks Beach

Kennebunkport

1. Grist Mill Property

This site, owned by Kennebunkport Conservation Trust, provides access to the Kennebunk River. A walkway runs down to a sturdy float appropriate for launching canoes and kayaks. Granite benches in the historic shape of mill parts and picnic tables are located near the ramp. The launch is open during daylight hours, and boaters will find better launch conditions near or on high tide.

Directions & Parking: From Dock Square, Kennebunkport, turn left onto Maine Street, continue onto North St, then turn left to the end of Mill Ln. Hand-carry boats may be driven to the property to be dropped off but no parking is available on-site. There is public parking at the fire station on North St. **Lat/Long:** 43.3647, -70.4784

2. Silas Perkins Park

This small park along the Kennebunk River overlooks a busy marina full of sail and motor yachts. The park, with picnic tables and benches, is a restful spot in the middle of a bustling summer resort area. Dogs are not allowed.

Directions & Parking: From Dock Square, Kennebunkport, turn right onto Ocean Ave, follow for about 0.2 mile between Arundel Yacht Club and the Yachtsman Motel. There is limited on-street parking on adjacent streets. The park is a short walk from the parking areas at the Dock Square shopping district. **Lat/Long:** 43.3580, -70.4751

3. Breakwater/Colony Beach

A mix of public and private ownership, this very popular, medium-sized beach is bisected by a large rock outcropping that is ideal for tide pool exploration. In addition to providing sand and ocean waves for beach-lovers, it's a good launch site for scuba divers and paddlers. The breakwater, constructed from boulders, offers a flat walking surface out into the ocean. Nearby businesses include restaurants and shops. There are no public restrooms at the beach.

Directions & Parking: From Route 1 in Kennebunk, turn onto Summer St/ME 35 and follow for 3.5 miles. Turn left onto Western Ave, then turn right onto Ocean Ave for about 1 mile. Across from Colony Hotel turn right to the beach. Limited parking is available adjacent to beach; there is additional parking on Ocean Ave in marked locations.
Lat/Long: 43.3472, -70.4743

Breakwater/Colony Beach

4. Parson's Way

This paved Ocean Ave walking trail offers dramatic ocean views, with numerous spur trails linking the road, the path and the water. The path provides access to the popular Blowing Cave and Spouting Rock areas and takes visitors by the Bush family's summer estate on spectacular Walker's Point. The complete walk from Dock Square along the Kennebunk River to Walker's Point is 4.8 miles. Summer traffic is heavy on the Ocean Ave.

Directions & Parking: From Route 1 in Kennebunk, turn onto Summer St/Route 35 and follow for 3.5 miles. Turn left onto Western Ave, and then turn right onto Ocean Ave. Limited off-street parking along Ocean Ave before St. Ann's Church.
Lat/Long: 43.3442, -70.4728

5. Spouting Rock 

Spouting Rock sends spray high into the air, providing a show of exploding salt water. Located along Parsons Way – with numerous benches positioned for the view – the attraction lures thousands of tourists each year. Walker's Point, the family retreat of President George H.W. Bush, offers a dramatic backdrop to the ocean's restless waves and pounding surf.

Directions & Parking: From Route 1 in Kennebunk, turn onto Summer St/ME 35 and follow for 3.5 miles. Turn left onto Western Ave, and then turn right onto Ocean Ave. The trailhead lies between 188 and 190 Ocean Ave, before St. Ann's Church. There is limited off-street parking. **Lat/Long:** 43.3417, -70.4682

6. Blowing Cave

This site lies along Parsons Way, a seaside walk that offers classic views of Maine's rock-bound coast. When waves roll in at high tide, surf crashes on ledges and flings mist into the air. Because of weathering, the sea cave does not produce spouts that are as showy as in the past, but tide and moon occasionally recreate conditions for the drama. The best view of the cave is near Walker's Point, facing west. With mild conditions, the rocks offer a scenic spot for a picnic.

Directions & Parking: From Route 1 in Kennebunk, turn onto Summer St/ME 35 and follow it for 3.5 miles. Turn left onto Western Ave, then turn right onto Ocean Ave. Follow for about 2 miles, to limited marked parallel parking.
Lat/Long: 43.3442, -70.4630

Blowing Cave

7. Cleaves Cove Beach

This secluded, rocky beach (with sandy patches) forms a curved cove offering some shelter to visitors. At low tide, pools form in rocky areas, inviting explorers to search for sea creatures and crabs. The large seawall of a private home plus beach vegetation offer some privacy from the nearby road and residential area. The Kennebunkport Conservation Trust owns this parcel; bathroom facilities and lifeguards are not provided; dogs are not allowed.

Directions & Parking: From Route 1, Kennebunk, turn onto Summer St/ ME 35 and go 3.5 miles. Turn left onto Western Ave and go 0.4 miles, then turn right onto Maine St for 0.5 mile. Bear left onto Wildes District Rd for 0.7 mile, then bear right onto Turbats Creek Rd for 0.5 mile. Continue on Ocean Ave/Shore Rd for 0.3 mile. Turn left onto Halcyon Way to the right-of-way at the end of the road. Access is extremely narrow and unloading is limited to 10 minutes. On-street parking is available on Ocean Ave. **Lat/Long:** 43.3515, -70.4497

8. Causeway Launching Area 

This part-tide gravel area, which lies next to a causeway connecting Trott Island in Cape Porpoise with a tiny island to the south, is best for kayaks and canoes. The site also offers shore fishing access to protected, calm waters.

Directions & Parking: From Route 1 in Kennebunk, turn onto Summer St/ME 35 and follow for 3.5 miles. Turn left onto Western Ave and go 0.4 mile; turn right to Maine St and go 0.1 mile; then turn left onto School St and go 2 miles. Continue onto Pier Rd for 0.5 mile. The launch, on the left just before the causeway, has very limited parking on the dirt shoulder past the causeway. **Lat/Long:** 43.3677, -70.4323

9. Goose Rocks Beach 

This 2-mile sandy beach, protected by a barrier reef (Goose Rocks), is known for soft sand that is ideal for walking and jogging. Two smooth, wide, inviting crescents face open ocean, with plenty of room to set up chairs and umbrellas, relax, swim and comb the shore for sand dollars. The beach is popular with families, paddlers who can launch hand-carried craft from the sand, and those who fish from shore. Birders can scout a marsh at the southeast end for wading and water birds. Summer cottages line the beach road and there is a general store nearby. There are no lifeguards or permanent restroom facilities on-site. Dogs are limited to early morning and later evening hours. Several public rights-of-way to the shore are located along Kings Highway between New Biddeford Road and Dyke Road. There is also a public right-of-way to the Batson River at the far west end of Kings Highway, though parking is very limited. Two portable toilets are located near the Dyke Road entrance.

Directions & Parking: From Dock Square, turn left onto Maine St and continue onto North St. Turn right on Beachwood Ave. Turn left on ME 9, then right on Dyke Rd. At the end of the road turn left and park in limited parallel-parking sites along King's Highway. Daily, weekly, and seasonal parking permits are available for a fee at the general store, town office, and public safety department. (A parking permit does not guarantee that a parking space will be available in the limited on-street parking areas.) There are no off-street lots. **Lat/Long:** 43.3984, -70.4103

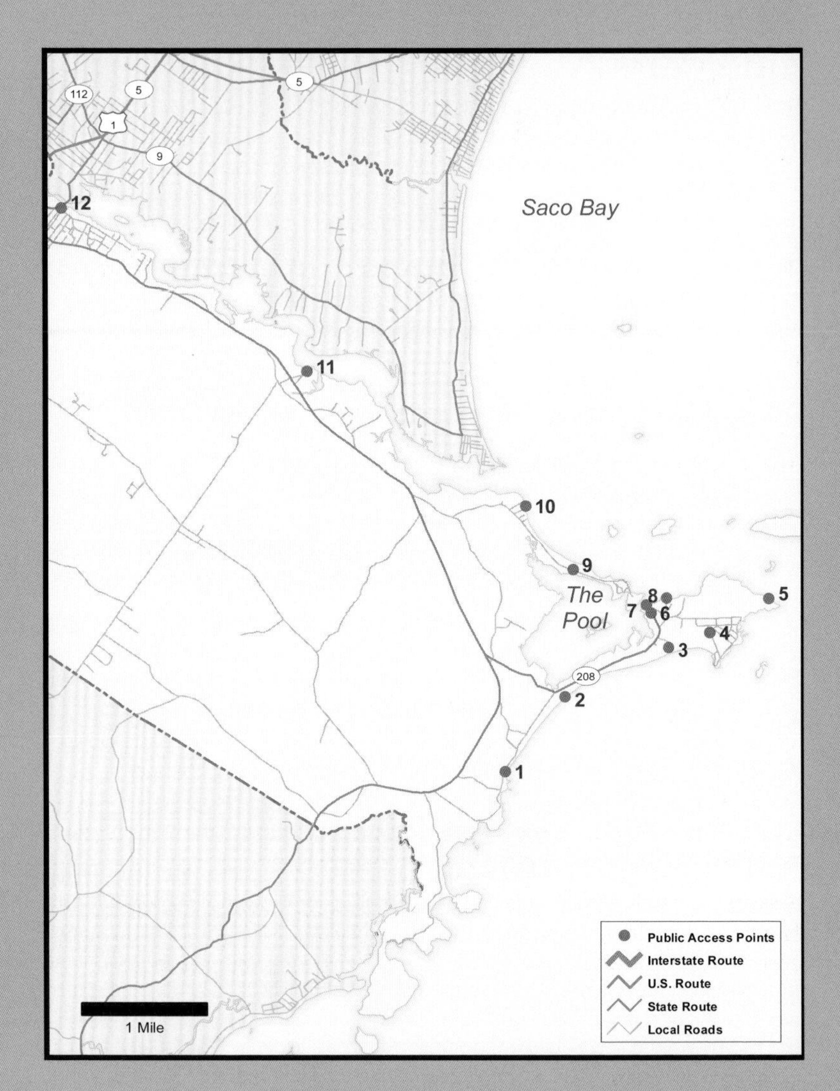

Biddeford

1. Fortunes Rocks Beach
2. Middle Beach
3. Gil Boucher Park
4. South Point Sanctuary
5. East Point Sanctuary
6. Yates Street Park
7. Vines Landing
8. Staples Street Beach
9. Park in the Pines
10. Hills Beach
11. Marblehead (Meetinghouse Eddy) Boat Launch
12. Mechanic's Park/White's Wharf

Biddeford

1. Fortune Rocks Beach

A 2-mile sandy beach fronting open ocean offers traditional beach activities. Reliable surf delights those who enjoy body surfing, skimboarding and kayaking. The unbroken and mainly level beach is ideal for walking and jogging on hard-packed sand. Birders look for shorebirds in migration and seek out Lily Pond's songbirds at the edge of the strand. The beach parallels the road, making it easy to access but less private. Lifeguards are seasonal. Portable bathrooms are provided. Dogs and horses are not allowed during the day from May to September. At other times of the year, dogs must be leashed and owners must collect waste. Visitors should, if possible, time a visit to avoid full high tide when the beach area is most restricted.

Directions & Parking: From downtown Biddeford take ME 208/ME 9/Pool St approximately 5 miles to ME 208/Bridge Rd. Continue on ME 208/Bridge Rd to Fortunes Rocks Rd and turn right to the beach, which has limited on-street parking. A seasonal parking permit is required (available from Biddeford City Hall) between June 15 and Labor Day. Overnight parking is not allowed. **Lat/Long:** 43.4273, -70.3772

2. Middle Beach

This long, sandy beach offers a flat, wide surface ideal for beach walks and jogging on firm, ocean packed sand. Wide enough to accommodate games and sand castles, this area also has classic shallow wading for young children as it gently slopes into deeper water. Seasonal lifeguards are provided, but there are no bathroom facilities. Dogs and horses are not allowed during the day from May to September. At other times of the year, dogs must be leashed and owners must collect waste.

Directions & Parking: From ME 208/ME 9/Pool St, bear left onto ME 208/Bridge Rd. At the intersection, go straight into a small parking lot. A seasonal parking permit is required (available from Biddeford City Hall) between June 15 and Labor Day; overnight parking is not allowed. **Lat/Long:** 43.4362, -70.3678

3. Gil Boucher Park

Also known as Biddeford Pool Beach, this area includes a big, sandy beach with grassy dunes that offer some privacy from nearby homes. The beach is ideal for swimming and other summer beach activities. Small-boat users may hand-carry and launch from the beach (difficult with large swells). The site offers seasonal lifeguards and bathrooms. Dogs and horses are not allowed during the day from May to September. At other times of the year, dogs must be leashed and owners must collect waste.

Directions & Parking: From downtown Biddeford take ME 208/ME 9/Pool St approximately 5 miles to ME 208/Bridge Rd. Continue on ME 208/Bridge Rd to Mile Stretch Rd and turn left. Travel 0.9 mile and turn right onto Gilbert Place to the parking lot. A seasonal parking permit is required (available from Biddeford City Hall) between June 15 and Labor Day. Overnight parking is not allowed. **Lat/Long:** 43.4424, -70.3517

4. South Point Sanctuary

This sanctuary is actually an access path, owned by Biddeford Pool Land Trust, that leads to beautiful Gil Boucher Park, a public beach. The path runs through woods and dunes, then on to a boardwalk to the beach. Birders find this area to be prime habitat for migrating shorebirds and wading birds. Dogs are not allowed.

Directions & Parking: From ME 208/ME 9/Pool St take slight left onto ME /208/Bridge Rd. At the intersection, turn left onto Mile Stretch Rd. Go 1.1 miles and merge onto Lester Orcutt Blvd. Turn right onto 1st St, then right onto 7th St. After a few houses, there will be a path on the right into the woods. There is limited parking on 7th St.
Lat/Long: 43.4440, -70.3448

5. East Point Sanctuary

Maine Audubon's 30-acre sanctuary on the eastern tip of Biddeford Pool offers visitors a wide, easy trail around the peninsula, plus paths down to the shore (but beware of steep, eroding shore banks and poison ivy throughout). The point looks directly out onto Wood Island Light, with a string of smaller islands to the west. Visitors can also see the sweep of sandy beaches that end in the Prouts Neck headland to the northeast. Birders consider East Point a "must stop" location; extending so far into the water, it's a good area for migration as well as unusual storm-blown species. Fishermen frequent the rocks on the rim of East Point. Dogs are not allowed; there are no bathroom facilities; visitors need to respect private land and posted rules.

Directions & Parking: From downtown Biddeford take ME 208/ME 9/Pool St approximately 5 miles to ME 208/Bridge Rd. Continue on ME 208/Bridge Rd. At the intersection, turn left onto Mile Stretch Rd. Travel 1.1 miles and merge onto Lester Orcutt Blvd. Pull onto the shoulder (very limited parking). The trail begins at the end of road.
Lat/Long: 43.4459, -70.3402

East Point Sanctuary

6. Yates Street Park

This small park, which overlooks the inner harbor, offers banks of wild rose bushes, benches, and a view of both yachts and commercial fishing boats – a slice of the dual life of every coastal village. It's a nice place to picnic or watch birds cruise around the harbor. The park is open from dawn to dusk; leashed dogs are allowed; owners must clean up after pets.

Directions & Parking: From ME 208/ME 9/Pool St, bear left onto ME 208/Bridge Rd. At the intersection, turn left onto Mile Stretch Rd. Go one mile, turn left onto Yates St, and go less than a mile to limited on-street parking on left. **Lat/Long:** 43.4461, -70.3546

7. Vines Landing

This park in the center of town provides a terrific view of Wood Island Light, whose stone tower rises above low vegetation and rock ledges on an island just offshore. A gravel boat ramp with slabs of concrete can support small trailers and light craft; paddlers may hand-carry as well. Anglers can fish from the shore or launch and try their luck in the pool or open water. Kayak rentals, a grocery store, shops and a post office are within easy walking distance. Those interested in a lighthouse tour can contact Friends of Wood Island Lighthouse. There are no bathroom facilities; leashed dogs are allowed.

Directions & Parking: From downtown Biddeford take ME 208/ME 9/Pool St approximately 5 miles to ME 208/Bridge Rd. Continue on ME 208/Bridge Rd to Mile Stretch Rd and turn left. Travel one mile, turn left onto Yates St and follow to minimal parking at the end. Overnight parking is not allowed. **Lat/Long:** 43.4471, -70.3552

8. Staples Street Beach

An access path, bordered by beach roses and other wild flowers, leads to a small, rocky beach with patches of white sand overlooking the outer harbor. At low tide there are a few large rocks ideal for sunning or picnicking. Because of limited parking, the beach is most often used by locals. Biddeford Pool Land Trust maintains the path and beach.

Directions & Parking: From ME 208/ME 9/Pool St bear left onto ME 208/Bridge Rd. At the intersection, turn left onto Mile Stretch Rd. Go 1.1 miles and take a sharp left onto Lester Orcutt Blvd. Take the second right onto Fairfield St. Turn left onto Staples St and follow it to the end. Limited parking is available on Staples St. **Lat/Long:** 43.4480, -70.3518

Staples Street Beach

9. Park in the Pines 

This small, scenic park along tidal Biddeford Pool offers birders access to tide pools, mud flats and a nearby marsh. Other visitors may picnic or sit on shaded benches to watch boats, people and wildlife. Paddlers can hand-carry and launch from a half-tide gravel ramp; low tide provides a muddy take-out, so timing can be important. The park is open dawn to dusk; there are no bathroom facilities; alcoholic beverages and unleashed dogs are prohibited.

Directions & Parking: From downtown Biddeford take ME 208/ME 9/Pool St approximately 4 miles to Hills Beach Rd. Go 1.6 miles; the park is on the right. Vehicles may enter to drop off kayaks or canoes but there is no parking lot. **Lat/Long:** 43.4510, -70.3670

10. Hills Beach

Located in a residential area near the University of New England on the north side of Biddeford Pool, this narrow, sandy beach at the outlet of the Saco River is most often used for fishing (from the jetty) and bird watching along nearby wetlands. The 500-yard stretch of sand offers some protection to beach-goers, which means a bit less wind and smaller waves. Occasional grassy dunes offer some privacy. Small-boat users may hand-carry and launch from the beach. There are no lifeguards or bathroom facilities. Dogs and horses are not allowed during the day from May to September. At other times of the year, dogs must be leashed and owners must collect waste.

Directions & Parking: From downtown Biddeford take ME 208/ME 9/Pool St approximately 4 miles to Hills Beach Rd. Go about 0.75 mile; the beach is accessible off side streets to the left. Limited parking is available on odd-numbered sides of the side streets; cars must face the direction of traffic flow. **Lat/Long:** 43.4585, -70.3746

Marblehead/Meetinghouse Eddy Boat Launch

11. Marblehead/Meetinghouse Eddy Boat Launch

This state-owned launch site, the most active on the river, has two well-constructed, all-tide ramps and a float that allows boaters to head down the Saco River for open water or tarry on the river to fish. (Striper fishing lures dedicated fishermen to the mouth of the Saco in early summer.) This site also offers excellent shore fishing access; anglers may cast from the grassy lawns. An outhouse is provided.

Directions & Parking: From downtown Biddeford take ME 208/ME 9/Pool St, about 2.5 miles to Marblehead Ln, where a brown sign marks the site. Upper and lower lots offer space for many vehicles and trailers. **Lat/Long:** 43.4739, -70.4099

12. Mechanic's Park/White's Wharf 

This attractive park on the shore of the Saco River offers an observation deck from which visitors can watch gulls wheeling high above and boats plying the river. Interpretive signs provide fascinating details for those interested in history. Landscaping and native flowers border the mowed area, inviting visitors to stay and picnic, or at least enjoy a moment of rest on the benches. Roller blading, skate boarding, ball games, and frisbee are not permitted. The park is open from dawn to dusk; there are no bathroom facilities.

Directions & Parking: From ME 9/Main St in Biddeford, turn onto Water St southwest of the Saco River. The park is immediately on the left. Parking is available on-street and in a city lot. **Lat/Long:** 43.4926, -70.4495

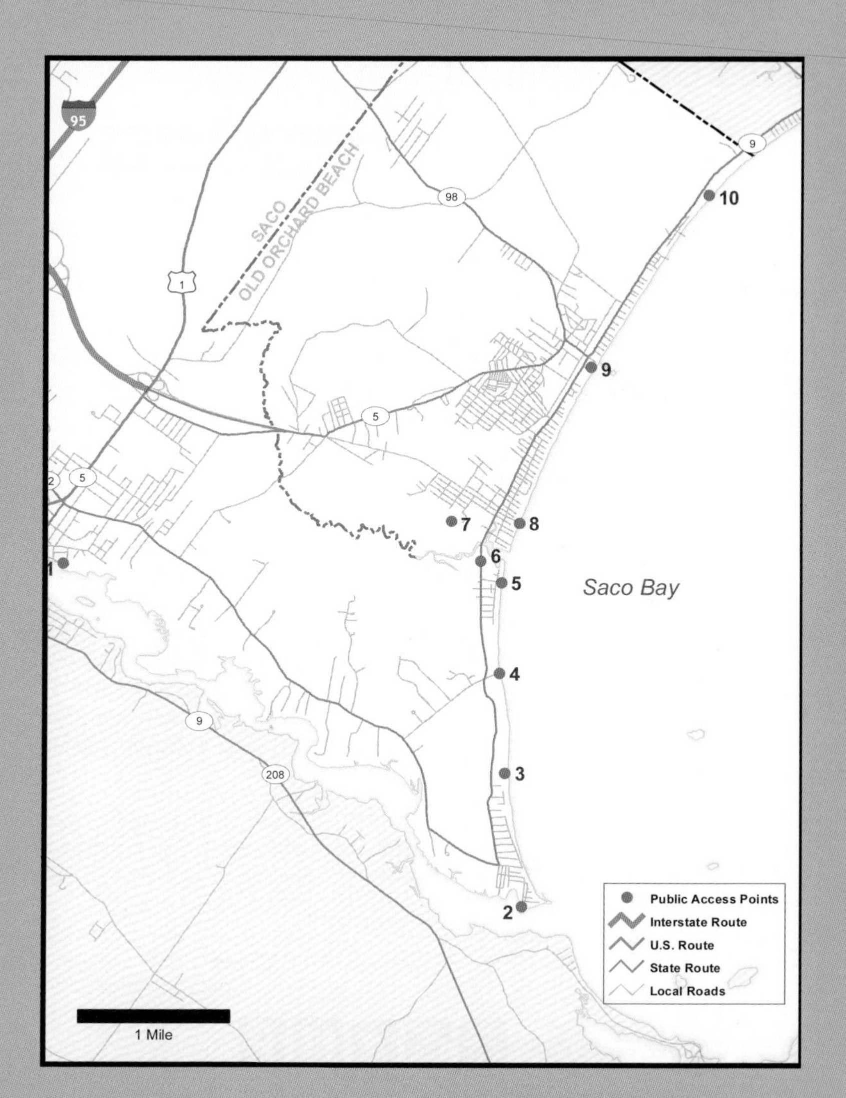

Saco-Old Orchard Beach

1. Saco River/Front Street Boat Launch
2. Camp Ellis
3. Ferry Beach State Park
4. Bay View Beach
5. Kinney Shores Beach
6. Goosefare Brook Wildlife Observation Platform
7. Ted Wells Memorial Trail
8. Ocean Park (Old Orchard Beach)
9. Old Orchard Beach
10. Surfside Beach

See next page for Saco-Old Orchard Beach Listings ➤

Saco-Old Orchard Beach

1. Saco River/Front Street Boat Launch

This site is located immediately below Cataract Dam, which forms the head of tide; the launch is on the eastern shore at what is locally called Meetinghouse Eddy. The dock and paved, full-tide ramp are suitable for all sizes of trailers, but boaters should exercise caution around the ramp at low water to avoid grounding. Shore anglers may follow the path along the river bank that leads to a popular fishing spot below the dam; information is posted regarding fishing access at the dam. Swimming is not allowed.

Directions & Parking: From Saco, take ME 9 south, turn onto Front St and follow to the end. A large lot accommodates vehicles and trailers. **Lat/Long:** 43.4948, -70.4429

2. Camp Ellis

This area, part of the city's seaside community at the mouth of the Saco River, includes a small beach (at half and low tide), boat launch, jetty, extensive seawall of granite blocks extending northward and moorings for sail and motor craft. The site offers excellent fishing from docks, beach and jetty; there's a bait store nearby. The paved boat ramp accommodates trailers, although larger boats need half-tide or higher conditions. Land-based guests can stroll along the long breakwater out to deeper water and visit the area's seafood restaurants, a lobster pound and a general store. Use of docks and floats is by permit. Full-service restrooms are open from May to September; for the rest of the year, there are portable bathrooms.

Directions & Parking: From Saco, go 4 miles southeast on ME 9/Beach Rd/Ferry Rd. When ME 9 goes left on Seaside, take the next right onto Camp Ellis Ave, then the next left onto Maine Ave. Turn right at the beach and continue onto North Ave to the parking lot. The town charges a fee for parking and an additional fee to launch a boat. Additional fee parking may be found at nearby Ferry Beach State Park. Public parking is also available in these locations: Camp Ellis Ave, Eastern Ave and Lower Beach Rd. **Lat/Long:** 43.4627, -70.3818

3. Ferry Beach State Park

This 123-acre park offers a beach, 1.4 miles of trails, and plentiful information about natural history. The undeveloped strand is protected by forest and wetland. The wooded trails – wide and level with boardwalks across wetlands – offer views of wetlands, ponds and a rare stand of tupelo (black gum) trees. Facilities include changing rooms, bathrooms and a newly constructed nature center. Maps and interpretive material are available at the parking lot; staff offer some guided programs. Leashed dogs are permitted on the beach from October 1 to March 31. The entrance fee includes parking.

Directions & Parking: From Saco, take ME 9 to Bayview Road north of Camp Ellis. Summer parking is prohibited on ME 9; winter on-street parking is allowed near park gates on Bayview Road or on ME 9. **Lat/Long:** 43.4756, -70.3843

Ferry Beach State Park

4. Bay View Beach

This white sand beach is part of the continuous expanse that curves around Saco Bay from Pine Point in the north to Camp Ellis in the south. Wide and either flat or gently sloping, it is ideal for spreading out blankets and chairs, swimming, beach combing for sand dollars and colorful shells, and – during quieter hours – watching birds scoop up scraps of dinner from the departing waves. Dunes and waving sea grass shelter part of the beach, providing some privacy; private homes run along another part of the beach. The site has seasonal lifeguards and bathroom facilities; leashed dogs are allowed.

Directions & Parking: From Saco take ME 9 south, then turn left onto Bayview Rd and continue to its end, where there is limited parking and where a right-of-way leads to the beach. A larger lot is located nearby at the intersection of Seaside Ave and Bayview. Overnight parking is not allowed. **Lat/Long:** 43.4851, -70.3852

5. Kinney Shores Beach

This sandy beach – a great destination for a bike ride given the limited parking available – lies on the south side of Goosefare Brook, south of Ocean Park. At low tide visitors may wade between the two beaches, but beware of rip tides. Lifeguards are not provided; leashed dogs are allowed.

Directions & Parking: From Ocean Park, take ME 9/West Grand Ave south, go over the bridge across Goosefare (becomes Seaside Ave) and take a left onto Dune Ave and follow to Oceanside Ave. Five rights-of-way lead from this road to the beach; limited parallel parking is available on side streets. **Lat/Long:** 43.4918, -70.3854

6. Goosefare Brook Wildlife Observation Platform

This wooden deck, encircled by vegetation, offers a limited view of the marsh and beach where Goosefare Brook empties into Saco Bay. A thousand-foot, wheelchair accessible, stone-dust path leads to a ramp and platform. There is no beach access from this site.

Directions & Parking: From Saco, go 3 miles southeast on ME 9/Beach Rd/Ferry Rd. Turn left on Bayview Rd and go 0.7 mile to Seaside Ave. Turn left, go 0.8 mile to a small off-street lot. Look for a path on the right. **Lat/Long:** 43.4959, -70.3878

7. Ted Wells Memorial Trail

This beautiful one-mile trail, named after a naturalist who appreciated salt marsh ecosystems, winds through white pines, red maples and cinnamon ferns, ending at a platform with benches overlooking the marsh at Goosefare Brook. Saco Bay Trails rebuilt this trail and added more than 300 feet of raised boardwalk, making it an excellent birding site. A kiosk and guides with detailed information about plants along the trail are available at the trailhead. The trail crosses property belonging to Camp Oceanwood and the Rachel Carson National Wildlife Refuge. As the trail originates at a children's camp, visitors must check in at the office before hiking the trail.

Directions & Parking: From downtown Saco, go north on Route 1 and then turn right on Ocean Park Road/ME Route 5. Proceed straight at the "Halfway Roundabout" intersection in Old Orchard Beach, where the road continues as Temple Ave. Continue on Temple toward Ocean Park over railroad tracks. Turn right on Royal St and continue to the end. Park at Camp Oceanwoods, immediately off of Royal St, before the camp office. Check in at the office. To reach the trailhead, go to the right of the camp's main building and look for the kiosk, which is by the woods left of the pool; sign in at the kiosk.
Lat/Long: 43.4997, -70.3916

8. Ocean Park (Old Orchard Beach)

Located south of the town of Old Orchard Beach in a residential summer community founded in the 1880s, this beach is considered part of the continuous 7 miles of Old Orchard. Southern portions of the beach, near the outflow of Goosefare Brook, are popular with fishermen casting from shore. Because this area often has a strong undertow, swimmers are advised to use caution. This beach is more steeply sloped and not as wide as other nearby beaches but is quieter and less commercial. In summer, dogs are not allowed between 10 a.m. and 5 p.m. There is convenient access to a general store, gift shops and restaurants.

Directions & Parking: From the Old Orchard Beach and pier area, follow West Grand Ave to four-way stop. Turn left onto Temple Ave and use limited on-street and side-street parking. **Lat/Long:** 43.4996, -70.3833

9. Old Orchard Beach 

A well-known summer resort colony and popular tourist attraction, Old Orchard has open ocean views and 7 miles of white, fine sand that connect to Scarborough's Pine Point Beach. This active town is an ideal destination for people, groups, and families seeking both a beach and destination with shops, restaurants, lodging, evening entertainment, arcade, games, rides, and a long pier with vendors. The beach itself has seasonal lifeguard stations, public restrooms and changing areas. Dogs are not allowed during summer between the hours of 10 a.m. and 5 p.m.

Directions & Parking: The beach lies off East and West Grand Ave/ME 9. The beach is accessible from many points along Grand Ave; visitors staying in the area may be close enough to walk from their accommodations. Parking is on-street with meters or in fee lots. Amtrak Downeaster provides seasonal service to a station that is within walking distance of the beach. **Lat/Long:** 43.5148, -70.3735

Old Orchard Beach

10. Surfside Beach

This long, wide, segment of beach is part of Old Orchard Beach's 7 miles of fine, white, sandy beach. Located east of the pier, this area has a quieter and more private atmosphere. In summer, dogs are not allowed between 10 a.m. and 5 p.m.

Directions & Parking: Parcher Ave and nearby streets offer public access with limited on-street parking. **Lat/Long:** 43.5315, -70.3587

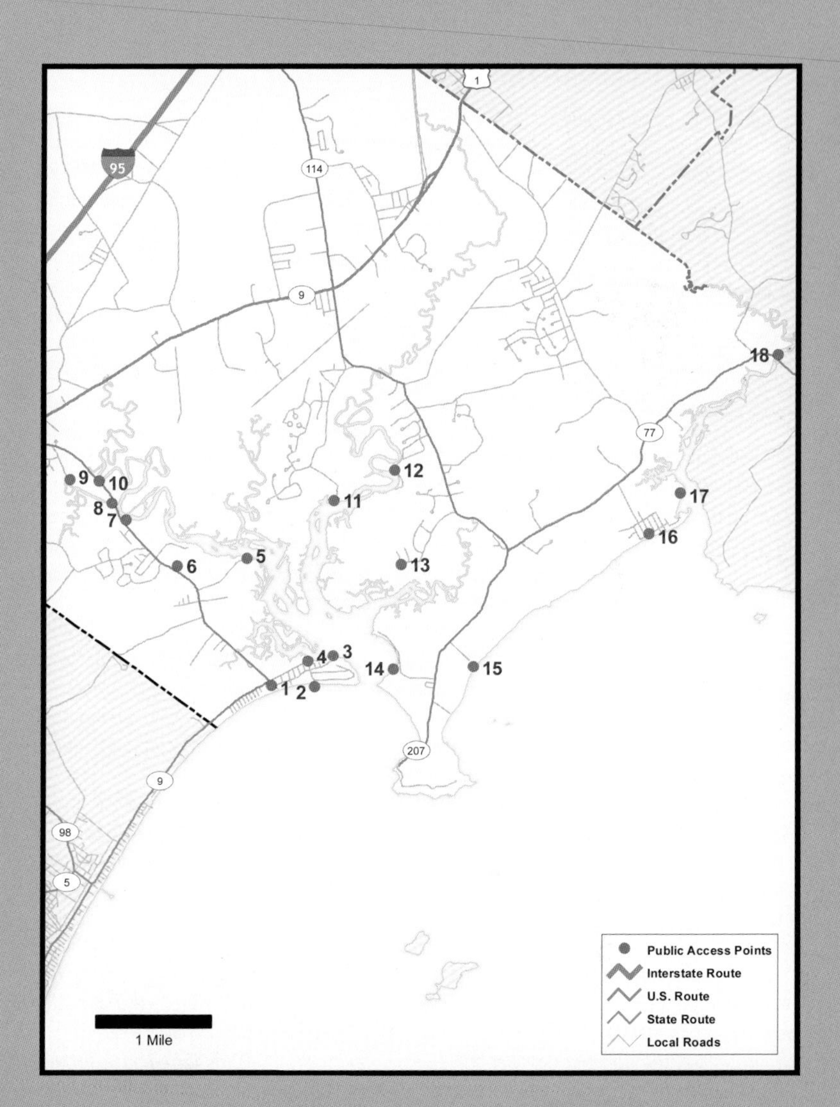

Scarborough

1. Snowberry Ocean View Park
2. Pine Point Beach
3. Pine Point Boat Launch
4. Avenue 5 Right-of-Way
5. Seavey Landing
6. Scarborough River Wildlife Sanctuary
7. Eastern Trail
8. Dunstan Landing
9. Dunstan Landing Road Right-of-Way
10. Scarborough Marsh Audubon Center
11. Winnock's Neck
12. Clay Pits/Nonesuch Boat Ramp
13. Old Neck Landing
14. Ferry Beach
15. Scarborough Beach State Park
16. Higgins Beach
17. Harmons Island Access
18. Spurwink River Fishing Pier

See next page for Scarborough Listings ➤

The Birds of Scarborough Marsh

Relatively few plants have adapted to living in or next to salt water. In Scarborough Marsh, the largest salt marsh in Maine, plants live in zones according to their ability to tolerate salt-water immersion. Black-grass congregates along the upper reaches of the salt-hay marsh, along with seaside goldenrod and sea lavender. In the high marsh, which floods during above-average tides, saltmeadow cordgrass dominates. From the lower marsh to just below mean high water – areas that the tide floods twice a day – salt pannes and smooth cord-grass are ever present. This variable habitat is perfect for numerous bird species, and the birders who eagerly follow them.

Migratory birds arrive, raise young and depart according to an annual schedule. Spring and fall migration are times of intense activity. Canada geese, with iconic black heads and white chin straps, arrive in huge flocks in March, looking for tender shoots of cordgrass. Green-winged teal, American black duck, mallard, blue-winged teal, and common and red-breasted merganser are common in both seasons; wood duck, northern pintail, American wigeon, and hooded merganser appear in smaller numbers.

The dabbling ducks (all of the above except merganser) putter in shallow water, tipping forward and rummaging with their bills in search of seeds, stems and leaves of emerging vegetation. Mergansers frequent deeper water, diving for fish but also taking crustaceans, aquatic insects, amphibians and other prey. Double-crested cormorants, horned grebes and common loons are regulars, often seen diving underwater in the marsh's channels, along with an occasional harbor seal.

If the marsh were a stage, herons would be the leading actors. These long-necked, long-legged birds move with elegance, rising in flight or darting forward to snatch unsuspecting prey (fish, amphibians, crustaceans, insects, even small mammals). Great blue herons, snowy and great egrets, and glossy ibis are fairly common to abundant in the marsh, arriving in April and leaving in September or October. Other wading birds that frequent the marsh include green herons, little blue herons, black-crowned night-herons, and tricolored herons. Many of these species nest on Stratton Island, a National Audubon sanctuary, located just offshore in Saco Bay. Look to the sky as the sun goes down, and you may see a large group flying south-west to roost on the island.

In late July through mid-October, shorebirds populate the mud flats, fattening up for the long trip south. Two dozen species, from the tiny least sandpiper to the stately whimbrel, draw birders to the marsh. Greater and lesser yellowlegs, semipalmated sandpipers, willets, and short-billed dowitchers are also among the most common shorebirds found here.

While salt marshes are most known for waterfowl, wading birds and shorebirds, the vast Scarborough Marsh supports a variety of other types of birds. It presents birders a unique opportunity to glimpse rare specialty sparrows. Nelson's sparrows are seen teed up on cord-grass along the Eastern Trail, making their distinctive hissing sound. This site is one of the best in the state to spot the elusive saltmarsh sparrow, and seaside sparrows have been seen on occasion. Raptors like bald eagles, northern harriers, red-tailed hawks and peregrine fal-cons can be seen soaring overhead. Tree swallows frequent birdhouses at the nature center; barn, cliff, bank and northern rough-winged swallows are seen as well. Herring gulls, great black-backed gulls and ring-billed gulls regularly fly above the marsh, stopping to sit on the high marsh surface or forage in the channel. In winter, rough-legged hawk, snowy and short-eared owls are possible.

With 3,100 acres of protected estuarine habitat, Scarborough Marsh accounts for 15 per-cent of the state's salt marsh. This rich environment provides valuable ecosystem services and serves as a productive habitat for a wide range of organisms. As a permanent home or tem-porary stopover ground for an assortment of avian species, Scarborough Marsh is a must-see and a sure delight for birders who visit the region.

Scarborough

1. Snowberry Ocean View Park

This tiny park, sandwiched between a residential neighborhood and a condo building, has benches, a water fountain, a foot shower and – best of all – access to Pine Point Beach.

Directions & Parking: From Route 1 in Scarborough, turn south onto Pine Point Rd and go 0.3 miles; the road ends at the park. There is no parking here; it's a drop-off area only. The nearest public lot is at Pine Point Town Landing (see separate description).
Lat/Long: 43.5407, -70.3436

2. Pine Point Beach 

This fine, long town beach stretches from Old Orchard east to the jetty at the mouth of the Scarborough River. Low tide uncovers an immense nearly-flat shelf of sand and a sandbar. This beach is perfect for walking, sunbathing, swimming and taking in the salt air. Anglers favor the jetty, especially when the stripers are running. Voice-controlled dogs are allowed from fall through late spring and for a few hours after sunrise during summer; leashed dogs are permitted in the evening. Horses allowed fall through spring; riders must have a permit.

Directions & Parking: From Route 1 in Scarborough, take Pine Point Rd south; turn left at the end onto East Grand Ave, then right onto Pine Point/King St. Turn right at Avenue 5. Park in the large town lot (fee) on Ave 5 off of King St. **Lat/Long:** 43.5406, -70.3365

3. Pine Point Boat Launch

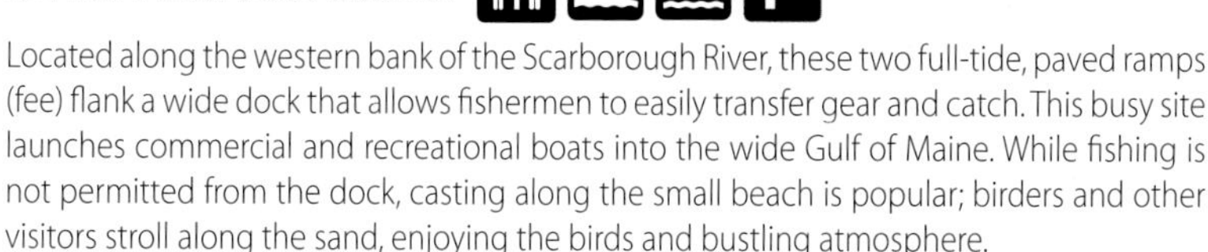

Located along the western bank of the Scarborough River, these two full-tide, paved ramps (fee) flank a wide dock that allows fishermen to easily transfer gear and catch. This busy site launches commercial and recreational boats into the wide Gulf of Maine. While fishing is not permitted from the dock, casting along the small beach is popular; birders and other visitors stroll along the sand, enjoying the birds and bustling atmosphere.

Directions & Parking: From Route 1 in Scarborough, turn south onto Pine Point Rd and go 0.3 miles; turn left onto Jones Creek Rd, which becomes Ave 6. Turn left onto King St; follow to very large parking area (room for many trailers) with public restrooms.
Lat/Long: 43.5445, -70.3334

4. Avenue 5 Right-of-Way

Clam diggers use this public path to get to acres of mud flats that form at low tide near the mouth of the Scarborough River. A lobster pound and restaurant are located nearby.

Directions & Parking: From Dunstan Corner, take Pine Point Rd to the end and turn left onto Jones Creek Rd. Follow Jones Creek to its intersection with Avenue 5. Park on street, following posted restrictions in summer. Cross the last driveway and walk along the path to the water. **Lat/Long:** 43.5438, -70.3378

5. Seavey Landing

This hand-carry site at the end of a residential road allows paddlers to launch into the Dunstan River at its confluence with the Scarborough River. This section of the marsh is notable because restoration efforts have largely reversed the damage caused years ago, when it was ditched and drained in an effort to combat mosquitoes. The changes may not be visible yet, but long-term the marsh will be a healthier with more diverse habitat for fish, birds, mammals and humans.

Directions & Parking: From Route 1 in Scarborough, turn south onto Pine Point Rd and follow for about 2 miles; turn left onto Seavey Landing Rd and follow to the end to limited off-street parking. **Lat/Long:** 43.5564, -70.3486

6. Scarborough River Wildlife Sanctuary 

Hikers, bird watchers, and pet owners can amble along 1.5 miles of trails in 52 acres of diverse habitat – upland fields and forest surrounding several spring-fed freshwater ponds, all leading down to salt marsh. Local teachers and students often use this area as an outdoor classroom. The sanctuary is open dawn to dusk; dogs must be leashed.

Directions & Parking: From Route 1 in Scarborough, go south onto Pine Point Rd; follow for 1.8 miles and pull into a very limited parking area on the left, across from a store. **Lat/Long:** 43.5553, -70.3606

7. Eastern Trail

This remarkable 2-mile footpath, which runs between Pine Point and Black Point Rds, takes visitors into the heart of Scarborough Marsh. People jog or bike here for a daily workout; birders stroll with binoculars in hand, scouting for a flick of the tail. The well maintained, gravel surface is stroller- and wheelchair-friendly. Shore fishing along the path is especially popular during striper season when the "schoolies" (small stripers) find food that a dropping tide sweeps toward them. Leashed pets are allowed; visitors should abide by posted rules, which are designed to protect the Scarborough Wildlife Management Area.

Directions & Parking: From the west: From Route 1 in Scarborough, turn onto Pine Point Rd and follow it for 1.2 miles to the parking lot on the left. From the east: From Route 1, go south on ME 207/Black Point Rd for 0.4 mile, turn right on Eastern Rd and follow to the end, where the trail begins. **Lat/Long:** 43.5609, -70.3698

Eastern Trail

8. Dunstan Landing

This site is a jumping-off spot leading into an enticing wildlife area, where visitors may see a hungry heron peering into a shallow pool before striking a fish with lightning speed, or hear red-winged blackbird sporting bright orange epaulets calling "Conk-la-ree! Hikers can head northwest on a half-mile trail through patches of scrub, coastal forest and salt marsh to the right-of-way at the end of Dunstan Landing Rd; this trail parallels Cascade Brook, site of a habitat restoration project. Or, they can turn south on a trail that parallels Pine Point Rd and connects to Eastern Trail, which in turn crosses Scarborough Marsh. Boaters can hand-launch at high tide and explore either the brook or river. (Visitors should be aware that parts of the path in the middle of the marsh may occasionally be flooded.)

Directions & Parking: From Route 1 in Scarborough, turn south onto Pine Point Rd. Follow for a mile and pull over at a sign and enlarged shoulder at the intersection of Cascade Brook, Pine Point Rd and the Dunstan River. **Lat/Long:** 43.5630, -70.3722

9. Dunstan Landing Road Right-of-Way

This path at the end of Dunstan Landing Rd follows a road that in the 1800s crossed Scarborough Marsh to Pine Point Rd. The path quickly changes from asphalt to dirt as it becomes more wild. The lush, tangled growth and edge habitat between forest and marsh attract wading birds as well as migrating songbirds. Paddlers can launch here at high tide, but it's a 600-foot carry to the water; Dunstan Landing is a better site from which to explore Cascade Brook and this section of Scarborough Marsh.

Directions & Parking: From Route 1 in Scarborough, turn south onto Pine Point Rd and follow for 0.2 mile, turning right onto Dunstan Landing Rd. Follow to limited parking at a turn-around at the end. **Lat/Long:** 43.5658, -70.3796

Scarborough Marsh Audubon Center

10. Scarborough Marsh Audubon Center

From Maine Audubon's Nature Center, located on a bend of the Dunstan River, visitors can hand-launch a boat, dip their paddles, and let the tide carry them – ever so quietly – within yards of a heron or egret. The center is open daily in the summer, running educational programs for all ages, offering interactive displays and exhibits, providing guided bird/wildlife tours by foot or canoe, and renting canoes and kayaks for those who prefer self-guided tours. For optimum wildlife viewing, paddling is best at half or low tide. A nature trail is available year-round.

Directions & Parking: From Route 1 in Scarborough, take Pine Point Rd south for almost a mile; the center is on the left. Park in the lot or along the road.
Lat/Long: 43.5657, -70.3745

11. Winnock's Neck

Clammers are the primary users of this public right-of-way at the end of a residential road.

Directions & Parking: From Route 1 in Scarborough, take ME 207/Black Point Rd south for about half a mile. Turn right onto Winnock's Neck Rd and continue for 1.3 miles, bearing right at a fork. Continue to the end, where there is no parking. **Lat/Long:** 43.5638, -70.3337

12. Clay Pits/Nonesuch Boat Ramp

This concrete, half-tide, state ramp, operated under lease by the municipality, is located on the eastern side of a switchback loop of the Nonesuch River, which meanders through Scarborough Marsh and empties into the Scarborough River. Commercial fishermen prefer the ramp at Pine Point, so paddlers and recreational boaters may find it easier to find parking here.

Directions & Parking: From the center of Scarborough at Oak Hill, turn right on ME 207/ Black Point Rd and go 1.6 miles. Turn right onto Clay Pits Rd and follow to limited parking with space for several trailers. **Lat/Long:** 43.5676, -70.3232

13. Old Neck Landing

This access, mostly used by clammers, leads to salt marsh and mud flats along the eastern part of Scarborough Wildlife Management Area. Paddlers can hand-carry, preferably at the top half of the tide. Birders, duck hunters and fishermen all use this access to enjoy abundant marsh wildlife.

Directions & Parking: From Route 1 in Scarborough, take ME 207/Black Point Rd south for 2.4 miles, turn right onto Old Neck Rd and follow to the end, where there is minimal parking. A short gravel path at the intersection of Old Neck Rd and Catherine St leads to **the shore. Lat/Long:** 43.5558, -70.3220

Old Neck Landing

Ferry Beach

14. Ferry Beach

This site on the eastern shore of the mouth of the Scarborough River provides activities for a variety of users. The wide, curving, white sand beach – fringed with small dunes, grass and beach peas – is an invitation to barefoot walks, sand castles and swimming from the gently sloping shore. (A jetty on the far side of the river protects this beach from larger ocean waves but at some tides the barrier can create a strong current that is dangerous for swimmers.) A concrete part-tide launch ramp mainly serves commercial fishermen. Recreational fishermen head to the ledge next to a navigational marker in their search for prime striper opportunities. Birders know that the sheltered cove and sandbars just offshore attract birds that feed on food exposed by low tide; in addition, some areas are fenced during summer to protect endangered piping plovers. Dogs are not allowed during the day in summer; at other times, rules vary but owners must always have (and most times use) a leash. There are separate fees to enter the park and to launch a boat.

Directions & Parking: From the center of Scarborough on Oak Hill, take ME 207/Black Point Rd south for about 4.5 miles. Turn right on Ferry Rd and follow to a large parking lot. Overnight parking is not allowed. **Lat/Long:** 43.5430, -70.3227

15. Scarborough Beach State Park

Water temperatures here regularly reach the high 60s in the height of the summer, prompting Scarborough to be touted as one of the best beaches in New England. This gorgeous strand runs almost one and a half miles northeast of Prouts Neck, providing lots of white sand for beachcombing and building castles. The view includes Richmond Island to the east, Bluff and Stratton Islands (the latter an Audubon Society sanctuary) to the south, and open ocean in-between. From the west end of the park, visitors can hike the cliff trail around Prouts Neck. Birders, looking for waterbirds, often prefer to visit in the winter. Swimmers are encouraged to remain in the designated area, which has lifeguards, to avoid rip-tide currents. Dogs not allowed spring through fall; they must be leashed the rest of the year.

Directions & Parking: From Route 1 in Scarborough, take ME 207/Black Point Rd south for about 4 miles; turn left into the park, where there is one lot near the gate and a second lot near the beach. **Lat/Long:** 43.5434, -70.3091

16. Higgins Beach

On a hot summer day this sand beach, maintained by the town and the Higgins Beach Association, is alive with family activity. Kites soar in the sky, balls bounce on the sand, toddlers squeal with delight, and teens park themselves on towels to sunbathe. Many people consider Higgins to be the best surfing beach in Maine, as waves set up far offshore and crest near land, but in summer surfing is not allowed from late morning through afternoon; when the activity is allowed, surfers must use leashes. Voice-controlled dogs are permitted from fall through late spring and for a few hours after sunrise during summer; leashed dogs are permitted in the evening. Portable toilets are located in parking lot.

Directions & Parking: From Route 1 in Scarborough, take ME 207/Black Point Rd south for 2.9 miles, then turn left on ME 77/Spurwink Rd and follow for 1.1 miles. Turn right on Ocean Ave and continue to the end. In summer, only accessible parking is allowed on-street (and there is a wheelchair ramp leading onto the beach); a municipal lot (fee charged) is located off Ocean Ave. **Lat/Long:** 43.5602, -70.2791

17. Harmons Island Access

Clammers use this right-of-way, which goes through brush and goldenrod next to a private yard, to gain access to productive mud flats. Others can use the path to walk down to this cove along the Spurwink River, with waving marsh grass and sparkling water.

Directions & Parking: From Route 1 in Scarborough, take ME 207/Black Point Rd south for 2.9 miles. Turn left onto ME 77/Spurwink Rd and go 1.1 miles. Turn right onto Ocean Ave, then left onto Greenwood Ave, which jogs right to join Harmons Island Rd. Pass three houses on the right. The small path starts after the driveway and leads to stone steps and the water. There is minimal parking. **Lat/Long:** 43.5653, -70.2739

Harmons Island Access

18. Spurwink River Fishing Pier

This quiet area, part of Rachel Carson National Wildlife Refuge, attracts paddlers, anglers, and visitors who seek a quiet moment by the river. Boaters can hand-carry across sand and rocks, then paddle to the river's mouth and back. Fishermen may cast along a thousand-foot stretch on the west bank, from the bridge north almost to an incoming stream. Others can use the wood observation deck to take in a slice of nature. Both refuge regulations (use non-lead jigs and sinkers only to prevent waterbird poisoning; attend lines at all times; carry out all litter including monofilament, which can be dangerous to wildlife; collect no bait fish) as well as Maine fishing regulations apply. User cooperation is important for the site to remain available; visitors should obey refuge rules and respect private property.

Directions & Parking: From Scarborough, go south on ME 207/Black Point Rd for almost 3 miles; turn left on ME 77/Spurwink Rd and follow for 3 miles to a small pullout on the left just before a bridge. Parking along the shoulder of Spurwink Rd is limited.
Lat/Long: 43.5827, -70.2574

Sand Beaches

There are many small pockets of sand scattered between rocky peninsulas along the Maine coast, however, what most people think of as beach systems—beaches with dunes—comprise only about 1% of the Maine coastline. Most are concentrated between Ogunquit and Cape Elizabeth (south of Portland) and in the Midcoast from Phippsburg to Georgetown at the mouth of the Kennebec River.

Why does this region have so much sand compared to the rest of the state? Three processes have contributed to this state of affairs: A continental glacier created and transported sediments to the general region (to what is now land as well as what is now covered by salt water); rivers and streams carried land-based sediment to their mouths; and currents, tides and wind have moved and sculpted both land-derived and offshore deposits.

In the last Ice Age, a continental glacier flowed from Canada across Maine and out to what is now the Gulf of Maine. The glacier eroded the bedrock, creating silt, sand and gravel. The glacier left bare rock in places and, in others, deposited sand and gravel. Upon its final retreat, the ice left large quantities of sediment in its wake in a variety of land forms including thick and gullied layers of clay, ridges of gravel, and flat sand plains.

Throughout Southern Maine, rivers and streams carried upland glacial sand to the coast, supplying beaches near the river mouths. Geologists think that before settling into its present course, for example, the Androscoggin River may have drained south, transporting sandy sediments from the interior and discharging them in Brunswick. Today, the joined Androscoggin and Kennebec Rivers supply sand to mid-coast beaches. From the rugged White Mountains of New Hampshire, the Saco River carried—and still carries—sand that forms beaches in Biddeford, Saco, Old Orchard Beach and Scarborough.

Along the shore, ocean waves, tides, and wind reworked and concentrated sandy glacial sediments to form beaches and dunes, particularly in bays between rocky headlands. From Ogunquit to the Kennebunks surf reworked glacial sand into strands of beaches over the last several thousand years. The process continues to this day: Rivers carry sediments to the ocean, where the elements move it from place to place in an annual cycle and over time.

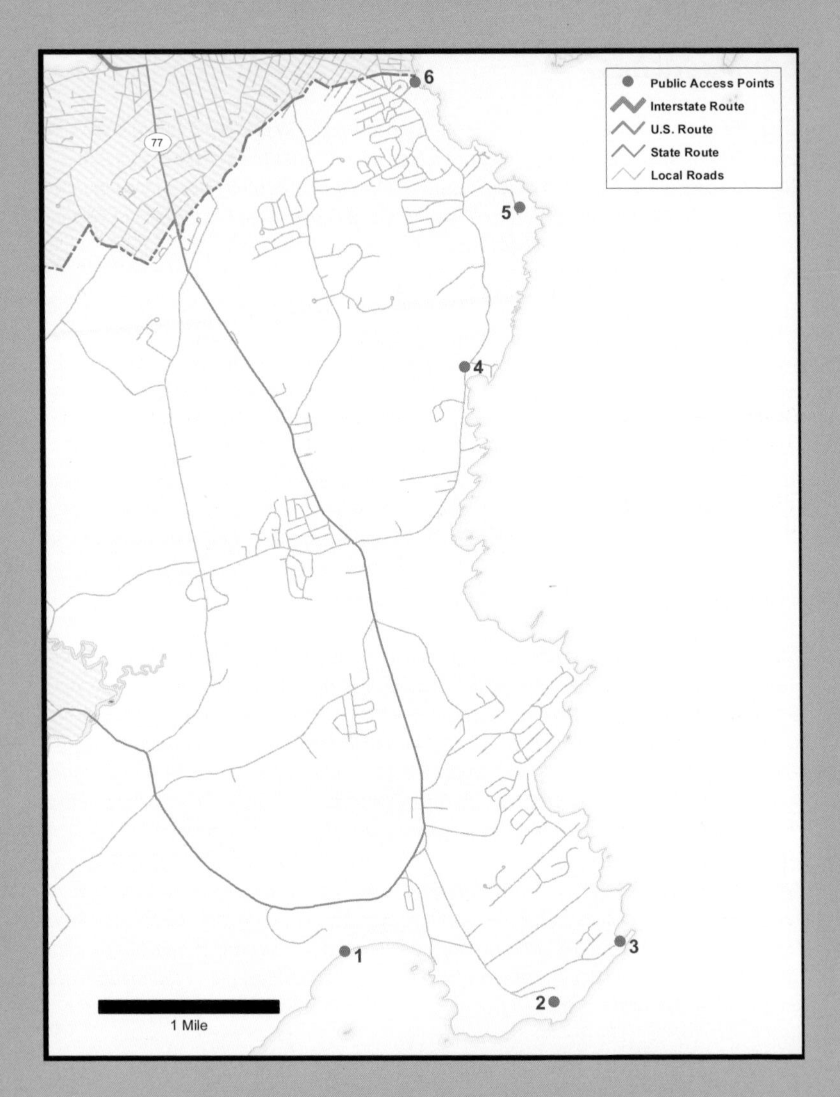

Cape Elizabeth

1. Crescent Beach State Park
2. Two Lights State Park
3. Dyer Point
4. Robinson Woods
5. Fort Williams Park and Portland Head Light
6. Cliff House Beach

Cape Elizabeth

1. Crescent Beach State Park, Cape Elizabeth

This 335-acre state park offers a wide, flat, mile-long sand beach that wraps around Seal Cove on the southern end of Cape Elizabeth. Most people come for the sand, relatively warm water, and generally light surf, but the park also offers a trail through spruce-fir forest and meadow and along the shore to quieter coves and ledges. Fishermen cast from the shore. Richmond Island, connected to the mainland by a rock jetty, lies along the southern horizon. The park (fee charged) is open year-round and has lifeguards in summer. In winter, visitors may hike, snowshoe or ski. Leashed pets are permitted on the beach October through March. Visitors must carry out litter; camping is not allowed.

Directions & Parking: From the junction of Broadway and ME 77/Ocean House Rd, take ME 77 south a little more than 5 miles and turn into a large parking at the sign. When the area is closed, park along ME 77. **Lat/Long:** 43.5637, -70.2291

2. Two Lights State Park, Cape Elizabeth

These 41 acres of dramatic, rocky headland – with salty breeze, crashing surf, and endless ocean – inspire awe throughout the year. Huge blocks, tattooed with bright yellow lichen, lay as if strewn on the ledges. Tide pools form at all levels, offering refuge for everything from sponges to brittle stars, sea stars, sea urchins and crabs. Wind-pruned pines and low-growing juniper testify to the strength of the wind. Even the grills and picnic tables here are tucked into nooks of shrubbery in order to provide protection from the elements. World War II batteries, situated to guard Casco Bay, give mute testimony of the past. Trails wind through the park, but most visitors come to scramble on the rocks, fish, picnic, or simply sit and watch the waves. An entrance fee is charged.

Directions & Parking: From the junction of Broadway and ME 77/Ocean House/Ocean Rd, take ME 77 south. Turn left onto Two Lights Rd and go a mile; go right at the fork onto Tower, continue to the end and park in a large lot. **Lat/Long:** 43.5599, -70.2057

Two Lights State Park

3. Dyer Point

This rocky finger stretching out from the easternmost shore of Cape Elizabeth offers a spectacular view of Casco Bay and the open ocean. The twin lighthouses, built in 1928, marked this dangerous shore for incoming ships. On a clear day, the eastern (automated) light is visible for 17 miles; the western light is now privately owned. Edward Hopper painted "Lighthouse at Two Lights" here. This area is of particular interest to birders who hope to see winter ducks. This Coast Guard property is licensed to the American Lighthouse Foundation (ALF). Please check with the foundation for times the property may be accessed.

Directions & Parking: From the junction of Broadway and ME 77/Ocean House/Ocean Rd, take ME 77 south. Turn left onto Two Lights Rd (stay left when road forks at Tower Rd) and go 1.7 miles to of-street parking at the end. **Lat/Long:** 43.5648, -70.1985

4. Robinson Woods, Sections I and II

These two properties, owned by the Cape Elizabeth Land Trust, encompass almost 145 acres of forest with a 1.4-mile loop trail through mixed hardwoods and pines on Section I and a mile-long trail past fields and waterfalls on Section II. Interpretive signs guide visitors as they walk through white pine, red oak and hemlock stands, some of which are more than 300 years old. The property also includes 2 acres of scenic waterfront on Pond Cove, just across the street. Because a freshwater stream flows into the cove, the water is less saline, sustaining more shoreline vegetation and providing greater forage for wildlife. In June, visitors often see eider moms and their young quite close to shore. At low tide, there is a cobble/sand beach, with seaweed-covered ledge at water's edge.

Directions & Parking: From South Portland, take Cottage Rd/Shore Rd south for 3 miles; park in a dirt pullout on the right. A short path through the woods leads to the beach. **Lat/Long:** 43.6107, -70.2164

5. Fort Williams Park and Portland Head Light

This 90-acre park combines two major features – a light commissioned by George Washington and a fort built in the late 1800s to protect Casco Bay and Portland Harbor – into a pleasant area with short trails along the water, shore fishing, picnicking, and scenic views of Ram Island Ledge Light and the islands of Casco Bay. The white tower and red-roofed white buildings of Portland Head Light are clearly the centerpiece. Visitors may visit the museum and gift shop or explore the old fort buildings, which were important during World War II and deactivated in 1963. Goddard Mansion, built in the 1800s, is also located within the park. In a winter with good snow, the park offers a rare treat – the opportunity to snowshoe or cross-country ski past a lighthouse. The site is open year-round, dawn until dusk.

Directions & Parking: From the junction of ME 77/Ocean St and Cottage St, take Cottage east (becomes Shore) 2.2 miles to the park entrance and park in one of the several lots. **Lat/Long:** 43.6235, -70.2104

Fort Williams Park and Portland Head Light

6. Cliff House Beach 

This small cobble beach is a gem. With limited parking and no facilities, it attracts fewer people, so it's a pleasant place to fish or contemplate the view across Danforth Cove to Cushing Island, with smaller House Island to the north and Peaks Island in the background. Beach pea, grasses, and shrubs form a buffer between the rocks and the upland trees. This town-owned site is open sunrise to sunset.

Directions & Parking: From the junction of Broadway and Cottage Rd (becomes Shore Rd), go south 1.2 miles; turn left onto Sea View and continue straight through a residential area for less than 200 feet to a paved path with stone steps that lead to the shore. There is limited on-street parking. **Lat/Long:** 43.6332, -70.222

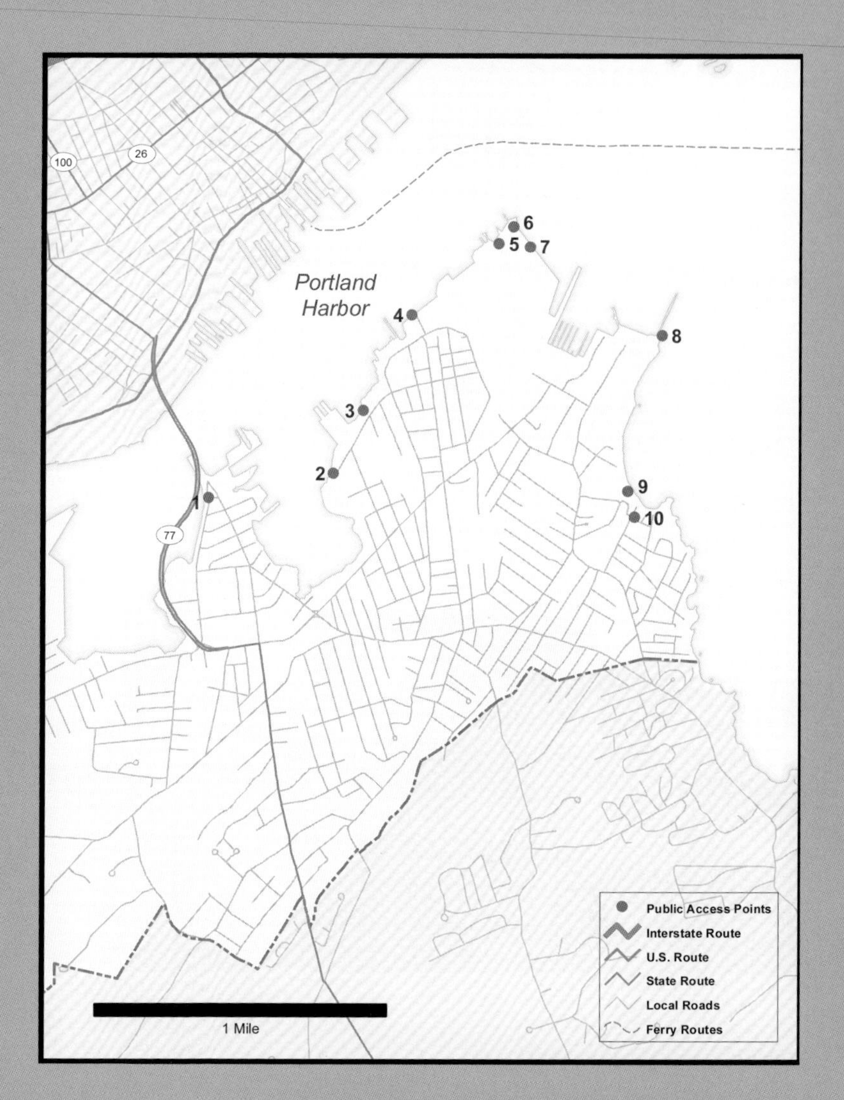

South Portland

1. Thomas Knight Park
2. High Street Right-of-Way
3. Davidson's Beach
4. Portland Street Pier
5. South Portland Municipal Boat Ramp
6. Bug Light Park
7. South Portland Greenbelt
8. Spring Point Ledge Light
9. Willard Beach
10. Spring Point Shoreway Trail

South Portland

1. Thomas Knight Park 

This small area next to and under Casco Bay Bridge is the part of the South Portland Greenbelt Walkway; here, a paved ramp leads up and over the bridge, connecting South Portland to Portland. Many commuters bike and even hike up the ramp to the bridge, enjoying harbor views and avoiding rush hour delays. For those who linger, shaded tables and benches overlook the bustling harbor. Sloping grassy areas lead to a cobble waterfront where hand-launching small boats is possible but not recommended; access leads into a very busy harbor with much larger boats. A town-owned landing facility includes a long pier and ramp to a float. Visitors who dock for more than a few hours must pay a fee, but that's plenty of time to tie up and walk to the Mill Creek shopping district for supplies or a meal. With the opening of the Casco Bay Bridge, Waterman Drive was redesigned for less intense use and it now hosts dedicated pedestrian sidewalks and shade trees.

Directions & Parking: From the Casco Bay Bridge or South Portland, take Broadway east. Turn left on Ocean St; go straight at the rotary, continuing on Ocean. Limited parallel parking is available on Waterman St where Ocean becomes Waterman. **Lat/Long:** 43.6416, -70.2558

Thomas Knight Park

2. High Street Right-of-Way

This public way includes a lush, vegetated path to a small pebbly beach. Local residents use the beach to fish, walk dogs, and enjoy the lovely views of the Portland waterfront, especially when the lights wink on at dusk. Boaters can hand-carry kayaks to the beach, but should be mindful that low-tide mud flats make launching mucky.

Directions & Parking: From the Casco Bay Bridge heading south, continue onto Broadway going east into South Portland. Turn left on Mussey St and follow to the end; turn left onto High St and follow it to the end, where there is limited parking and the path to the shore.
Lat/Long: 43.6429, -70.2473

3. Davidson's Beach

This public right-of-way offers a path and stairs to a small gravel beach with an excellent view of Portland Harbor. Open dawn to dusk, the beach extends from the Centerboard Yacht Club to the U.S. Coast Guard station.

Directions & Parking: In South Portland, from the Casco Bay Bridge, take Broadway east. Turn left on Pine St and then left on High St. Park on the street or continue straight to Pine St for more parking. **Lat/Long:** 43.6460, -70.2453

4. Portland Street Pier

This public pier located next to the Sunset Marina and Saltwater Grille is a working wharf where trucks drive on and off, lobster traps are stacked for use, and access to most floats used by commercial fishermen is gated and locked. Still, visitors may enjoy strolling along the wharf, catching the views of the islands of Casco Bay and taking in the bustle of the marina.

Directions & Parking: From the Casco Bay Bridge take Broadway east into South Portland. Turn left onto Sawyer St. At the end of the street turn right and then quickly turn left onto Portland St, following it to limited off-street parking at the end. There is no trailer parking.
Lat/Long: 43.6507, -70.2421

5. South Portland Municipal Boat Ramp

This public boat ramp (fee charged) next to Bug Light Park is designed to launch all types of recreation boats into the Fore River at the harbor's western edge. Two full-tide concrete ramps flank a double-wide dock system that allows for efficient boat handling during busy summer hours. Popular shore fishing extends from the dock area to Bug Light Park. When the mackerel are running, area children balancing rods on their bikes flock to this dock area.

Directions & Parking: From the Casco Bay Bridge in South Portland, take Broadway east almost to the end. Turn left onto Breakwater Dr and then right on Madison St. Follow Madison to its end, where there is a very large lot with room for many trailers.
Lat/Long: 43.6543, -70.2362

6. Bug Light Park

This 8.8-acre park, located at a former World War II shipbuilding complex, offers a variety of activities as well as views of Portland Harbor, the city's skyline and the bay's islands. Boaters can use a very busy paved public ramp (fees in season) to gain access to Casco Bay. Walkers can use a paved water-side path that connects to the South Portland Greenbelt Walkway. Fishermen can drop lines either off the paved walkway to the lighthouse or the rocks fronting open ocean. History buffs can explore Cushing's Point House Museum and the memorial to the Liberty Ships that were once built here. This park has well maintained lawns, a large field ideal for games and picnics, and plentiful benches at the edge of the water; bathrooms are located near the launch ramp. Portland Breakwater Lighthouse, also called Bug Light, marks the northern tip of land.

Directions & Parking: From the Casco Bay Bridge in South Portland, take Broadway east. Just before the end of the road, turn left onto Breakwater Dr and then right on Madison St; follow Madison to its end at a large parking lot.
Lat/Long: 43.6551, -70.2352

Bug Light Park

7. South Portland Greenbelt

This paved bicycle and pedestrian path connects South Portland parks and neighborhoods from the Wainwright Recreation Complex to Bug Light Park and the Spring Point Shoreway. The greenbelt, several miles in length, passes through the South Portland Mill Creek shopping district and residential areas, but it also winds near the water where only beach roses and late season goldenrod border the trail. Visitors may eat fresh bagels while dangling their legs over rocks at Bug Light, swim at Willard beach, or refresh themselves with iced coffee at Mill Creek shops. The greenbelt is part of the East Coast Greenway and crosses the Casco Bay Bridge, linking to the award-winning Portland Trails system and its refuges, trails, and bike paths – a remarkable blend of urban, coastal and neighborhood trail systems that allow users to travel from South Portland to Falmouth.

Directions & Parking: Parking is available at the Mill Creek shopping center, Wainwright Recreation Complex, and Bug Light Park (see directions Bug Light). To reach Wainwright Recreation Complex, take Highland Ave from the center of South Portland and head west. Turn right onto Gary Maietta Parkway and continue to the parking area.
Lat/Long: 43.6542, -70.2341

8. Spring Point Ledge Light 

Adjacent to Southern Maine Community College's campus, Spring Point Ledge Light's unique position at the end of a 900-foot breakwater jetty makes it the only lighthouse of its type accessible to the public. On the shore side of the lighthouse a path with benches and well maintained lawns follows the waterfront past Fort Preble's imposing granite battlements. The path also fronts a rocky beach where swimmers can find patches of sand to spread their blankets. Fishing from shore and the jetty is popular here, especially when the mackerel are running thick in the harbor. People enjoy strolling over the jetty's sturdy blocks for dramatic views of Fort Gorges on Hog Island Ledge; children delight in exploring Fort Preble's shaded secrets. In summer the Spring Point Ledge Light Trust opens the 1897-era lighthouse for weekend tours. Restaurants, shops and a full-service commercial marina are located nearby.

Directions & Parking: From the Casco Bay Bridge in South Portland, take Broadway east and turn left onto Preble St. Take the second left onto Fort Rd and follow it to the end. Park in available lots; some of the college's lots may be used when the college is not in session.
Lat/Long: 43.6499, -70.2254

Spring Point Ledge Light

9. Willard Beach

Willard is a 4-acre sand beach that links Fisherman's Point and Southern Maine Community College. It has a front-row seat on the main route into Portland Harbor, providing visitors with a view of a steady stream of ocean liners, catch-laden commercial boats and recreational boats as well as area landmarks such as Spring Point Light, Fort Preble, Fort Gorges and islands of Casco Bay. This site is part of the Spring Point Shoreway, allowing beachgoers to combine sand and sun with an easy walk to explore Fort Preble and Spring Point Light. Paddlers can hand-carry and launch from firm sand. The site also has a playground, seasonal bathrooms and a snack bar.

Directions & Parking: From the Casco Bay Bridge or South Portland take Broadway east into South Portland. Turn right on Preble St, then left on Willow St. Park in a large lot on Willow St or in some of the lots at Southern Maine Community College (down Fort Rd to its end) when the school is not in session. **Lat/Long:** 43.6423, -70.2272

10. Spring Point Shoreway Trail

This paved, 1.6-mile trail, which is both stroller and wheelchair friendly, passes through the Spring Point Marina to the shaded campus of Southern Maine Community College, then on to the Spring Point Arboretum and finally to Spring Point Ledge Light. At the light, a rocky beach with occasional patches of sand connects the shoreline to the more expansive, white sand of Willard Beach. The trail appeals to history buffs because it passes Portland Harbor Museum and the imposing, granite battlements of Fort Preble. This trail is one segment in an unusual urban, coastal and neighborhood system that allows users to travel from South Portland to Falmouth. This area is popular with dog walkers, who often send their furry friends for a swim at the lighthouse beach.

Directions & Parking: From the Casco Bay Bridge in South Portland, take Broadway east and turn left on Preble St, then take another left onto Willard (or, take Broadway and turn left onto Pickett St and right onto Madison). Parking is available at Bug Light Park or Willard Beach.
Lat/Long: 43.6414, -70.2267

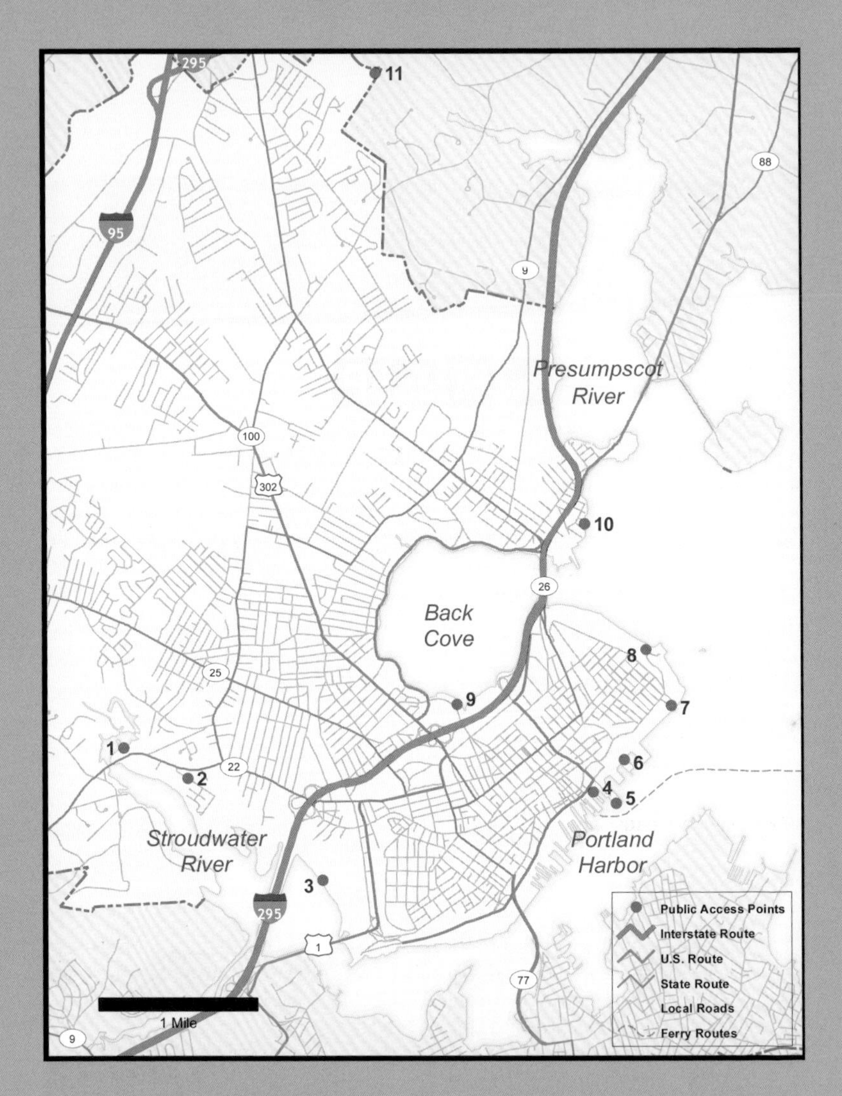

Portland

1. Fore River Sanctuary
2. Fore River Trail
3. Fore River Parkway Trail
4. Bell Buoy Park
5. Maine State Pier
6. Moon Tide Park at Ocean Gateway
7. Fort Allen Park
8. Eastern Promenade
9. Back Cove Trail
10. Kendall Street Right-of-Way
11. Presumpscot River Preserve

Portland

Fore River Sanctuary

1. Fore River Sanctuary P

This 85-acre wildlife sanctuary offers opportunities for hikers, bikers, skiers and snowshoers. From the Congress Street trailhead, the route follows the flat towpath of the Cumberland and Oxford Canal for more than half a mile before turning north across a wetland. It later joins the Fore River and a hilly loop leading to Jewell Falls, Portland's only natural waterfall. Red oak and white pine provide songbird habitat; lowlands where freshwater and salt marsh mingle attract birds. The site has kiosks with interpretive information as well as benches with views of the river's densely vegetated shoreline. The area is open from dawn to dusk; leashed dogs are allowed. A short excursion along Congress St links this area with the Fore River Trail and Stroudwater Trail as well as the Capisic Brook Trail.

Directions & Parking: From the south: Using the Frost St entrance, park in the Maine Orthopedics lot on 1601 Congress St and follow a trail into the sanctuary. From the north: Take Brighton Ave to Rowe or Hillcrest Aves and park at the end of the street. Or, enter from Starbird Ln to the east; again, park at Maine Orthopedics. See the Portland Trails website for details and further information. **Lat/Long:** 43.6604, -70.3093

2. Fore River Trail

This scenic path, which links to the Fore River Parkway, offers lush fields, singing red-winged blackbirds and vibrant riparian wetlands. A gravel trail with boardwalks runs along the river and rail tracks, through woods and marshes east to Thompson's Point. Signs along the way describe the area's fragile ecosystem and damage caused by an oil spill in Portland Harbor in 1996. To the west, a short walk along Congress St connects hikers to the Stroudwater Trail and the Fore River Sanctuary, an unusual opportunity to experience coastal nature sites and Portland's famous eateries on the same hike.

Directions & Parking: From I-295 in Portland, take exit 5 onto ME 22/Congress St West, merging onto Congress. Go 0.8 mile; turn left on Hobart St (and an immediate left to stay on it). Park along Hobart; the trail crosses over the street to the south. **Lat/Long:** 43.6578, -70.3012

3. Fore River Parkway Trail 

This 1.3-mile-long, paved urban walking trail along the river runs from the bus and train station at the Portland Transportation Center to Danforth St, passing Mercy Hospital and its Mercy Pond Loop. (The loop offers excellent birding as migrators converge on a green oasis in an urban landscape.) The trail ends abruptly on West Commercial St amid highways and heavy industry. Cyclists and walkers should use caution until sidewalk improvements in this area are complete.

Directions & Parking: From I-295 in Portland, take exit 5A onto ME 22/Alternate Route 1/ Congress St. Go straight through the intersection onto Thompson's Point Rd. Fee parking is available at the Transportation Center, 100 Thompson's Point Rd off Congress St.
Lat/Long: 43.6484, -70.2837

4. Bell Buoy Park 

This tiny public landing is the drop-off and pick-up location for water taxi services to the Casco Bay islands. Although there is a year-round floating wharf, unattended boats are not allowed.

Directions & Parking: Coming from the south, take I-295 to exit 4. Continue straight at the light and follow Commercial St for 1.9 miles. The park is on the right, just before the Casco Bay Lines terminal and parking garage. Park in metered on-street spots or in the garage. From the North, take I-295 to Exit 7 (Franklin Arterial.) Follow Franklin St to Commercial St. The park is directly on the other side of Commercial. **Lat/Long:** 43.6575, -70.2498

5. Maine State Pier

This extensive pier in Portland Harbor supports the Casco Bay Islands Transit District's ferry terminal as well as tiny Compass Park. Ferries that serve the islands operate year-round, ceasing operations only for severe storms. There are also scenic summer cruises (these include music cruises, private charters and lobster bakes); music from a wedding held on a chartered ferry can sometimes be heard drifting across the harbor. Boaters may tie up at the pier for short periods at the attached public wharf and dock; commercial, passenger-carrying schooners also berth on floating docks here. Despite all the activity, there's plenty of room to fish at the end of the concrete pier. Compass Park, open space on the pier itself, is occasionally a venue for concerts and festivals. Pedestrians may watch pier activity from benches, then venture into the cobblestone streets of the Old Port to find a rich assortment of eateries and shops.

Directions & Parking: From I-295, take Exit 7 for Franklin Arterial. Follow Franklin St to the intersection of Commercial St and Franklin St; the pier is located at 56 Commercial. Use the on-site parking garage or, as the pier lot is often full, on-street metered parking and parking garages in the Old Port. **Lat/Long:** 43.6560, -70.2469

Maine State Pier

6. Moon Tide Park at Ocean Gateway 

Architects designed Ocean Gateway (a terminal in Portland Harbor for ferries and cruise ships) to resemble the prow of a ship; the sleek building overlooks a park, pier and inner harbor waterfront. The park is not well signed but it is an inviting space with benches, newly planted trees and lawns, all of which lead to a high berm along the water. At high tide, it is possible to climb down to the water to fish. Portland's restaurants and shops can be found farther east on Commercial St.

Directions & Parking: Go northeast on Commercial St past Franklin to the junction of Commercial and Hancock Sts. The park is adjacent to the Ocean Gateway pier and event center. There is minimal parking in a small lot; more parking is available in city garages or at on-street meters. **Lat/Long**: 43.6598, -70.2459

7. Fort Allen Park

An extension of Eastern Promenade, this 9.3-acre park offers sweeping views of Portland Harbor, Casco Bay islands, wind-driven sailboats, and majestic cruise ships. The shaded promontory is rich with military history: The park was named for Revolutionary War hero Ethan Allen, who captured Fort Ticonderoga in 1775; a granite bench dedicated in 1929 honors the Union army; the giant mast of the U.S.S. Portland, commissioned in 1933 as a U.S. Navy cruiser, is housed here. While much of the Eastern Prom is busy and active, this quiet site invites serenity and contemplation – except on the Fourth of July, when it is the prime spot for viewing Portland's fireworks.

Directions & Parking: From I-295 in Portland, take exit 8, ME 26/Washington Ave south and take the first left onto Eastern Promenade. Follow this road until it turns southwest; Fort Allen is located at the corner. Park in a small turn-out lot. **Lat/Long:** 43.6652, -70.2401

8. Eastern Promenade

This 68-acre recreation complex offers something for everyone. East End Beach, the city's only public beach, provides several hundred yards of sand for family-oriented swimming. Nearby lie two half-tide paved boat launches (fee) that accept all trailer sizes as well as hand-carried boats. Fishermen cast from the docks and rocks and a grassy hillside park with benches and spectacular views of Casco Bay. A playground, ball fields and tennis courts offer some of the most scenic free recreation in Maine. The Eastern Promenade Trail, a 2.1-mile path with several side trips (including Loring Memorial and Fort Allen) connects to both the Back Cove Trail and the Bayside Trail, making this area ideal for biking, walking and running. The Maine Narrow Gauge Railroad Museum is also located on the Eastern Promenade.

Directions & Parking: From I-295 in Portland, take exit 8, ME 26/Washington Ave south and take the first left onto Eastern Promenade, where there are lots in the beach/launch area and on Cutter Dr (ample trailer parking). There is also parallel parking along the street.
Lat/Long: 43.6699, -70.2434

Eastern Promenade

Eastern Promenade

Back Cove Trail

9. Back Cove Trail

This flat, 3.5-mile loop around a tidal basin, marked every quarter mile, attracts thousands of walkers, runners and bicyclists and is a popular location for organized events, including spectacular fireworks. Some sections are paved and others are surfaced with stone dust. Visitors use the many benches that line the shaded trail, which is at its finest in the spring when trees bloom. Back Cove offers habitat for water fowl and wading birds that work the mud flats during low tide. Baxter Boulevard, which parallels the trail, is lit at night so the area is used long after sunset, with the city's illuminated skyline creating a dramatic backdrop.

This trail joins the Eastern Promenade Trail at Tukey's Bridge and it abuts two other recreation areas. Back Cove Park is a community space with a soccer field. Across the cove, Payson Park provides an opportunity for families to spread out on lawns for picnics and cool sea breezes. There are soccer and softball leagues, pick-up basketball and a sledding hill. Bathrooms available at both parks. Dogs must be leashed.

Directions & Parking: From I-295 in Portland, take exit 6B to Forest Ave. Turn right on Baxter Blvd, and then take another right onto Preble St. Turn into parking lot on the left. Large parking lots off Preble St and Elm St and on north side of Baxter Blvd at Payson Park.
Lat/Long: 43.6648, -70.2672

10. Kendall Street Right-of-Way 

This public access leads to a rough sand beach framed with sea grass and beach peas. The sandy path, located behind a guard rail, leads past attractive plantings of day lilies, daisies and roses to a sturdy stairway that descends to a wide-decked platform with chairs overlooking the beach. Overall, this is a place for seaside relaxation. It is possible to launch a kayak or canoe, although low tide reveals mud flats that make for mucky launches and landings.

Directions & Parking: From I-295, take exit 8 onto ME 26 north/Washington Ave; take the first right onto Veranda St; take the third right onto Richmond St; immediately veer right onto Kensington St. Pass under the interstate; turn left onto Berwick St; go left onto Windsor Terrace. Take the first right onto Lennox St and then left onto Kendall. Go to the end, where the right-of-way is located. Use on-street parking. **Lat/Long:** 43.6814, -70.2513

11. Presumpscot River Preserve

This beautiful preserve offers well maintained paths and clear signage on 48 wooded acres. The trail starts in a residential neighborhood and follows a deep ravine into dense vegetation. The trail is occasionally very steep; boardwalks and bridges cross wet areas. At the Presumpscot, signs direct visitors either up or downstream, with both directions offering spectacular views, rugged rock outcrops and lush vegetation. Downstream, on property protected by the Falmouth Conservation Trust, the trail goes to Presumpscot Falls, where a marked portage directs boaters around a small gorge and swift rapids flowing into salt water. Upstream, the trail offers short loops in wooded uplands but essentially follows the river's edge until crossing under the highway overpass. The preserve is popular with joggers, hikers and mountain bikers. Several smooth ledges that extend into the river invite quiet contemplation. Visitors should respect abutting private property and obey all signs.

Directions & Parking: In Portland, take Allen Ave to Summit St; turn right on Curtis Rd. Turn right at Overset Rd and park at the end of the street, as signs indicate.
Lat/Long: 43.7218, -70.2785

Portland as a Port City

The Wabenaki called it Machigonne, "Great Neck," describing the Fore River's most prominent feature. When the English arrived in the early 1600s, their orientation was toward the ocean and they saw Great Neck's potential as a port. One attempt at settlement, called York, failed; another, Casco, succeeded and grew into a trading and fishing village. The Massachusetts Bay Colony took charge in 1658, changing the name to Falmouth. The name lasted through the Revolutionary War, though the town itself was destroyed periodically – 1676, 1690 and finally 1775, when British ships sailed into the harbor and bombarded it. Three-quarters of the buildings, all wood, succumbed to fire. After the war, two municipalities were formed, Falmouth and Portland, the latter receiving the land along the harbor.

Many towns along Maine's coast became international ports with thriving ship-building and commercial markets. Portland in particular benefitted from its large, protected harbor and proximity to Boston. In 1853, a rail line that linked Portland with Montreal turned Portland into a major economic player. With the St. Lawrence frozen, goods destined for Canada arrived in Maine to be shipped north along what was eventually called the Grand Trunk Railway. Grain from Canada's heartland likewise debarked from Portland to feed the cities of England and Europe.

The demand for longshoremen grew just as the Potato Famine in the late 1840s prompted thousands to flee Ireland looking for work and a new life in a new land. Irish men found jobs on Portland's docks, loading and unloading goods.

During the political build-up to the Civil War, the federal government took steps to protect Maine's chief port, extensively rebuilding Fort Scammel on House Island and Fort Preble in South Portland. In 1858, workers began construction of Fort Gorges on Hog Island Ledge; the project was finished six years later. (Ironically, development of long-range rifled canon during the war left the three forts vulnerable to attack.) Despite the fortifications, Lieutenant Charles Read of the Confederate Navy slipped into the harbor in 1863 and made off with an armed revenue cutter. He was caught, but only because he couldn't find the ship's stash of munitions, which were hidden in a secret location.

In 1866, fire ripped through Portland's commercial district, destroying 1,800 buildings and leaving thousands homeless. As it was rebuilt – this time with brick – Portland became a city with fine Victorian mansions and a commercial district.

Portland's maritime light began to fade, however, as Canada opened its own ports. The city thrived during World War II, when it was the center for an array of military installations in Casco Bay, but the conclusion of the war brought relative quiet. More recently, with the waning of what were considered unlimited stocks of fish, the city's fishing fleet has also declined.

Portland, ever the phoenix, has resurrected itself, reassessing its relationship with the sea and redefining its identity as a port city. Waterfront redevelopment now focuses on balancing traditional use – the iconic working waterfront filled with fishing fleets and cargo ships -- and establishing Portland as a destination for visitors arriving by land or sea.

The Maine State Pier serves not only as the launching pad for ferry service to the Casco Bay islands, but a place frequented by folks fishing for mackerel and a landing for summer festivals and music. From Ocean Gateway, cruise ship passengers can walk east along the Eastern Promenade to take in spectacular views of Casco Bay, or west where they can wander along the waterfront catching a glimpse into the lives of resident lobstermen, scallopers and ground fishermen.

Portland is one of the busiest seaports in New England, handling everything from cargo to international passengers arriving by cruise ship. It's clear that history, culture and recreation will continue to intersect here for years to come.

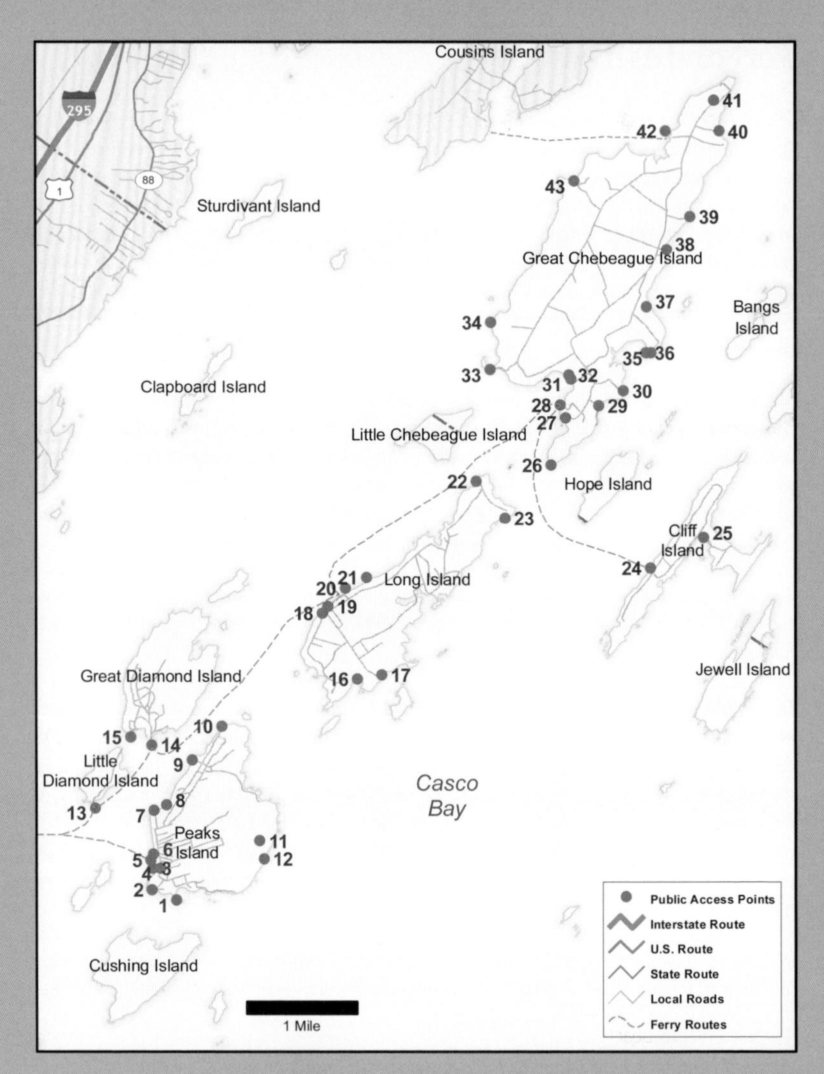

Casco Bay Islands

1. Picnic Point
2. Sandy Beach
3. Engineer's/Government Pier
4. Peaks Island Loop
5. Forest City Landing
6. Dinghy Beach
7. Centennial Street Ramp
8. Centennial Beach
9. Trefethen Ave Right-of-Way
10. Evergreen Landing
11. Battery Steele
12. Back Shore
13. Little Diamond Ferry Landing
14. Great Diamond Island State Pier
15. City Road Sandbar Right-of-Way
16. Wreck Cove
17. South Beach
18. Front Beach
19. Ponce Landing
20. Mariner's Landing
21. Town Boat Ramp
22. Cleaves Landing
23. Eastern Avenue Right-of-Way
24. Cliff Island Public Wharf
25. Dinghy Beach
26. Deer Point
27. Bennett Cove Right-of-Way
28. Chandler Cove Landing
29. Higgins Farm
30. Jenks Landing
31. Chandler Cove Beach
32. Ancient Burying Ground at the Belvin Property
33. Indian Point Conservation Easement
34. Sunset Road Right-of-Way
35. Waldo Point Right-of-Way
36. Waldo Point
37. Rose's Point Beach
38. Central Landing Right-of-Way
39. Fenderson Road Right-of-Way
40. Soule Road Right-of-Way
41. The Gray Path
42. Stone Wharf
43. Division Point Right-of-Way

Casco Bay Islands (Peaks Island, Little and Great Diamond Islands, Long Island, Cliff Island, Chebeague Island)

1. Picnic Point

This rocky point on the south side of the island offers great views of a protected, blue-water cove as well as endless open ocean. Patches of pebble and sand beach dot the shore, which leads to a sand bar that divides Haddock and Ryefield Coves. The bar extends to a tiny island thick with tangled bushes and wind-stunted trees. At low tide, the area, with tide pools and rock ledges, is ideal for picnics and shore exploration.

Directions & Parking: From the ferry, take the first right onto Island Ave, the first left onto New Island Ave, the second right onto Whitehead, and the first right onto Hadlock Cove Rd. The point is on the right as the road curves to the north; a path leads to the site. Another path leads from Long Point Rd to Picnic Point. There is on- street parking. **Lat/Long:** 43.6509, -70.1947

2. Sandy Beach

This popular local beach, screened with grasses, wildflowers and shrubs, is best used at low water because it's quite narrow at high tide. On hot summer days, families set up lawn chairs, children dip in and out of shallow wading areas and kayakers slip in and out of the cove – even though the beach has more rocks than sand. At one end, a set of sloped rocks offers an ideal place to stretch out and enjoy the ocean view. More bikes than cars can be accommodated at this location.

Directions & Parking: From the ferry landing, turn right on Island Ave, take a right on Greenwood St, and at its end turn right. There is minimal on-street parking. A wooden stairway and ramp lead to the water. **Lat/Long:** 43.6521, -70.1992

3. Engineer's/Government Pier 

This long pier and dock mix public and commercial use and offer short-term dockage. The beach has shallow, sloping access to the water. On the north side of the pier there is a municipal dinghy beach.

Directions & Parking: The pier is located immediately south of the ferry terminal on Welch St and can be accessed through the ferry lot, where parking is available.
Lat/Long: 43.6550, -70.1988

4. Peaks Island Loop

Peaks offers bicyclists and amblers 15 miles of flat, paved roads that run from the rugged, rockbound waterfront through tranquil, residential neighborhoods. Brisk salt breezes; a rocky shoreline fringed with lupine, beach peas, and wild roses; small coves for swimming and tide pool exploration; benches along the water with views of lobstermen hauling traps and sailboats heeling into the wind – it's all there. Visitors should remember that although island traffic is slow and relatively minimal, the roads are narrow and merit careful navigation.

Directions & Parking: A ferry ride of 20 minutes puts visitors at the wharf on the western side of the island. To bike the official loop, go up the hill to the first intersection; turn right onto Island Ave and go 0.2 mile to the second right (Whitehead St, but it's unmarked). Go 0.25 mile and take the second right onto Seashore Ave (marked) and follow to its end. Turn left onto Trefethen Ave and go 0.1 mile down a steep hill. Turn left onto Island Ave to return to the ferry.
Lat/Long: 43.6554, -70.1978

5. Forest City Landing 

Casco Bay Lines ferry lands at this large, public dock that includes a ramp and float that are available for fishing and temporary boat tie-ups. Water taxis deliver passengers and supplies to this location.

Directions & Parking: The landing is on the southwest side of the island, at the end of Welch St. There is a parking lot just up the street. **Lat/Long:** 43.6555, -70.1996

6. Dinghy Beach 

This small sand and pebble beach, located on the west shore of the island, is a good place to launch paddle boats and small craft because it slopes gently into Casco Bay. Kayak tours and rentals are available here. A commercial wharf, next to the beach, has launching facilities for large boats.

Directions & Parking: From the ferry landing, turn left onto Island Ave. Access the beach either before or after the market. On-street parking is available. **Lat/Long:** 43.6568, -70.1991

Dinghy Beach

7. Centennial Street Ramp 

This wide, concrete, half-tide boat ramp can accommodate any size trailer. Paddlers can launch from the ramp or from granite blocks on either side, and small, sandy patches of beach provide sites for swimming and wading. The ramp looks across to the Diamond Islands.

Directions & Parking: The ramp, located at the corner formed by Centennial St and City Point Rd, has limited parking on the shoulder. **Lat/Long:** 43.6625, -70.1991

8. Centennial Beach 

This white sand beach, better at lower tide when more beach is exposed, is lovely for swimming; its shallow, sandy areas are ideal for wading and young children's water play. Beach goers can enjoy views of nearby islands, diving seabirds and sailboat races.

Directions & Parking: From the end of Centennial St turn right and follow signs; there is limited on-street parking. Take a short path to the beach. **Lat/Long:** 43.6632, -70.1968

9. Trefethen Ave Right-of-Way

This public site, which is adjacent to the island's private boat club and looks west to Great Diamond Island, offers access to the beach and water south of the building at the end of the road.

Directions & Parking: From the ferry, take the first left onto Island Ave and follow it north (at 0.3 mile, turn right, then take second left to stay on Island). Trefethen is 0.7 mile on the left. Park on Island (not Trefethen) Ave. **Lat/Long:** 43.6692, -70.1923

10. Evergreen Landing 

Visitors can reach this small but popular sand beach from a wooden stairway that leads through a wall of wild roses. This family area has excellent wading and shallow, safe swimming; it's a great place for water toys, kayaks and beach exploration. Adventurers can easily wade across a sandbar to offshore rocks at low tide.

Directions & Parking: From the ferry, take the first left onto Island Ave and follow it north (at 0.3 mile, turn right, then take second left to stay on Island). Go to the northern tip of the island, where the road becomes Evergreen Landing Rd. The landing is on the left as Evergreen turns east. There is limited on-street parking. **Lat/Long:** 43.6736, -70.1869

11. Battery Steele

During World War II this battery, at the mouth of Portland Harbor, was the most important fortification in Casco Bay. Each of its two 16" guns – triangulated by observation towers on Peaks, Jewell, Cushing and Bailey Islands – could shoot a 2,240-pound shell nearly 26 miles at enemy battleships or submarines. Years later, when the site was threatened by development, island activists formed the Peaks Island Land Preserve to purchase the property and conserve it as open space. Although the battery provides no direct access to the water, this reminder of the past does provide sweeping ocean view.

Directions & Parking: Visitors are encouraged to go by foot or bicycle; a path from Seashore Ave passes through a marsh and along a pond. The battery can also be reached from Brackett Ave, a dirt road, where on-street parking may be available. **Lat/Long:** 43.6587, -70.1798

12. Back Shore

This 1.5-mile scenic section of the eastern shore is located along the island's loop road and Seashore Ave. Many people walk or bike the route, stopping to relax, eat and read on easily accessible rocks and ledges. The rocky beaches are lovely for picnicking and sight-seeing, with dramatic open ocean views of islands and sailboats. Tide pools form at low water, offering opportunities for exploration. The rocky shore and ocean swells make the area inappropriate for swimming. The City of Portland owns this popular destination.

Directions & Parking: From the ferry landing, walk up the hill and turn right onto Island Ave. Follow it 0.2 mile; take the second right (Whitehead St, unmarked); go 0.25 mile and take the second right onto Seashore Ave. Follow Seashore to right when road forks at Maple. The Back Shore stretches to the northeast. **Lat/Long:** 43.6564, -70.1789

Back Shore

13. Little Diamond Island Ferry Landing

This ferry dock has a long pier with a private shelter where passengers may wait out rough weather. The pier offers expansive views of Casco Bay islands, the ferry's transit, and large summer homes thickly screened by shade trees and gardens. A connected floating dock is a public landing that offers dinghy tie-ups. Swimmers may walk out the long pier to the dock and leap in the bay's icy waters to cool off.

Directions & Parking: The landing is at the south end of the island, at the end of Cityview Rd. Although the roads are available to public foot and bike traffic, no larger motor vehicles are allowed on the island and all the properties beyond the roadways are private.
Lat/Long: 43.6634, -70.2102

14. Great Diamond Island State Pier

This large dock where the ferry lands has a wide ramp for loading and unloading vehicles and cargo as well as an attached float that is limited to quick service tie-ups. Commercial fishermen also use this site to load and unload gear, so it has more of a rugged, working Maine atmosphere than the Diamond Cove Ferry Landing.

Directions & Parking: From the ferry terminal, take Diamond Ave southwest for 0.6 mile. Veer left onto Cleeve. At the second fork, bear left on Summit; Valley joins from the left. Go straight onto Nancy Ln/Nichols St to the end at the terminal. Limited parking is available at the end of peninsula where the dock begins; there is a large lot for golf carts.
Lat/Long: 43.6710, -70.1996

15. City Road Sandbar Right-of-Way

At low water, the bar between Great Diamond and Little Diamond Islands is a "city road" with public right-of-way. Paddlers and islanders with light trailers launch here when the bar is mostly submerged, using the old road as a ramp (and using care because of the unpaved surface); the return must be timed for similarly high water in order to avoid a low-tide carry. On both islands, there are small beach areas beside the road, and children enjoy wading on the road/sandbar. As the tide affects all of these activities, visitors should keep an eye on its progress and beware of strong currents.

Directions & Parking: From the ferry terminal, go south on Diamond Ave for about half a mile, veering left at fork onto Cleeve St. At the next fork, stay on Cleeve, then take the first left onto Spring (it jogs left and becomes Bay) to the water. **Lat/Long:** 43.6723, -70.2034

16. Wreck Cove

If a boat were blown on shore here, it would not fare well – or at least that's how it seems on a windy day when waves from the south pound the cobbled beach. The Town of Long Island owns this wild, 11-acre wooded parcel with 400 feet of shoreline. There is some seaweed-covered sand, but it doesn't invite sunbathing. Instead, this is a beach for watching waves and wildlife, or catching a few moments of solitude.

Directions & Parking: From the ferry, go south on Island Ave and take the second left onto Beach Ave. Go a little more than half a mile and turn right on Wylie St. Park on Beach Ave and follow the clearly marked path through the woods to the shore.
Lat/Long: 43.6800, -70.1626

17. South Beach

This area – also known as Sandy Beach – is tucked behind Vaill Island, which provides protection from waves and on-shore breezes. The combination of gentle sand and gentle waves is an unbeatable attraction. In summer, umbrellas, lawn chairs, and sand castles dot the strand. The beach starts at a jumble of wave-smoothed rocks and ledge near the end of the road and swings northeast between a stand of beach grass and the water. Beach-goers should take care to avoid poison ivy, a shrub with leaves composed of three shiny leaflets (in the fall and winter, there may be clusters of cream-colored berries), which grows with other trail-side shrubs. Part of the beach is private; visitors are asked to respect posted signs.

Directions & Parking: From the ferry, go south on Island Ave. Take the second left onto Beach Ave and continue to its end. Park along the road. **Lat/Long:** 43.6806, -70.1580

18. Front Beach

This narrow beach snakes between a line of homes and the water so it's not a secluded area, but it does provide lovely views out to Great Diamond, Cow and Clapboard Islands. The beach faces northwest, so it's protected from summer on-shore breezes.

Directions & Parking: This beach is located off Island Ave – on the northern shore of the island – just south of the Island Ave/Beach Ave intersection. A small rock with "Beach Path" painted on it (located near a general store and next to parking signs), marks the access trail. There is limited parking along Island Ave. **Lat/Long:** 43.6885, -70.1690

19. Ponce Landing 

This long wooden pier makes a nice perch for catching the breeze and watching the island's comings and goings – the ebb and flow at the ferry terminal to the north, the constant stream of residents to the Post Office to the east, and beachcombers exploring Front Beach to the south. A ramp and float lie at the end of this public-access pier.

Directions & Parking: From the ferry, go south to Island Ave; take the first right (opposite Garfield St) just before the Post Office and follow to the pier. Park on the road.
Lat/Long: 43.6894, -70.1680

20. Mariner's Landing 

The Casco Bay Lines ferry lands here, making this site the hub of the island's activity. The state owns the public wharf; the town owns the attached floats. There's a small building to provide shelter for those waiting for the ferry.

Directions & Parking: The wharf is located on Wharf St, along the northwest side of the island. It shares parking with the town hall that lies across the street. **Lat/Long:** 43.6913, -70.1647

21. Town Boat Ramp 

A gravel road leads to this all-tide, concrete, trailerable launch site. A ramp and small float are located to the side. Even those who don't intent to launch a boat can sit on the dock, dangle feet in the water, and enjoy the view of Little Chebeague, Clapboard Island and the mainland.

Directions & Parking: From the ferry, go north on Wharf Ave; at the "T" go left to the ramp and pier, where there is limited off-road parking. **Lat/Long:** 43.6932, -70.1611

22. Cleaves Landing

This small beach, set off from the road by two granite benches, looks west to Little Chebeague Island. It's a lovely, quiet place to swim, lounge on the sand or picnic. Boats are moored close to shore and lobster traps are sometimes stored in the grassy area above the beach. There's private land to the north and south; please respect private property.

Directions & Parking: From the ferry, take Island Ave north to its end, turning left at the "T" and going straight to the water, where there is limited parking along road.
Lat/Long: 43.7060, -70.1415

23. Eastern Avenue Right-of-Way

This town right-of-way leads through goldenrod and sumac to streaked ledge with thickets of juniper and rugosa rose with its large, rose-purple flowers. It's a gorgeous spot, looking across Luckse Sound to Cliff Island and due east to Hope Island. The rugged, rocky shore precludes swimming and launching boats; visitors can simply enjoy the view and whatever treasures have been washed up by the sea.

Directions & Parking: From the ferry, take Island Ave north to its end. Turn right at the "T" and go to the turn-around circle at the end of the road, which has limited parking.
Lat/Long: 43.7012, -70.1362

24. Cliff Island Public Wharf

This large dock, located on the western shore facing Luckse Sound, serves the Casco Bay Lines ferry. A sheltered waiting/storage area is located on the wharf; a ramp and float are attached on the north side. There's a store and seasonal café nearby.

Directions & Parking: The wharf is at the end of Wharf St, off Sunset. Parking for golf carts is located nearby. **Lat/Long:** 43.6949, -70.1096

25. Dinghy Beach

This sand and pebble beach is located along the southern shore of the "H" formed by Cliff Island. It looks southwest across a beautiful cove, bordered by rock promontories on each side, to the open Atlantic in the distance. Dinghies are pulled up on the beach; boats come and go from moorings in the cove.

Directions & Parking: From the ferry, follow Wharf Rd, cross Sunset Ave, then turn left onto Church Rd. At 0.5 mile, take the second right onto Island Ave. The beach is on the right, along Island Ave/Beach Rd. **Lat/Long:** 43.6991, -70.1000

26. Deer Point

The Chebeague and Cumberland Land Trust holds an easement on 13 acres at the southern tip of the island, providing a stunning panoramic view of Luckse Sound, Long Island, Little Chebeague and the mainland. The parcel lies along the seaward side of a steep, rocky ridge that defines this end of the island. Says the Trust: "It's as close as we come in Casco Bay to the typical 'Downeast' island, with only a strip of gray ledge separating its thatch of dark spruce from the ocean." The 2 acres at the point – a pocket of sand, fingers of ledge, rugosa rose and woods – are designated "forever wild" and protected from all development. Neither fires nor overnight camping is allowed.

Directions & Parking: From the Chandler's Cove Landing go to South Rd. Deer Point Rd (marked Western Landing Rd on the town map) lies on the opposite side of the intersection. Park vehicles and bikes on South, as Deer Point Rd is for pedestrians only. Although it's only 0.25 mile long, the last part is slow going; the road turns into a rough path that descends over the ledges to the shore. **Lat/Long**: 43.7084, -70.1280

27. Bennett Cove Right-of-Way

This town right-of-way leads to a small beach with a finger of rock nicknamed "The Nubble." The cove looks out onto a tiny island with Long Island beyond; a barge provides access for loading and unloading boats.

Directions & Parking: From the Casco Bay Lines Ferry landing, follow the road to a "T" Turn right onto Bennett Cove Rd and continue to the end. Parking is very limited due to the barge landing; park on South Rd. **Lat/Long:** 43.7144, -70.1255

28. Chandler Cove Landing 

This large state-owned wharf, located on the southern shore of Chandler Cove, provides access to and from Portland and other Casco Bay islands. Recreational fishermen may cast their lines from the wharf between ferry landings. A town float, attached to the wharf, provides tie-ups for smaller craft and access for lobstermen.

Directions & Parking: The wharf is located at the end of Chandler's Cove Landing Rd. Park in the lot. **Lat/Long:** 43.7160, -70.1265

29. Higgins Farm

The shorefront of this old island farm is open to the public. Beach lovers can swim and settle into the sand; paddlers can hand-carry to the water; commercial fishermen can launch from here; and when berries are ripe, anyone can pick them. The view is out onto Luckse Sound, with Hope, Cliff and Stave Islands spread across the horizon. This recreational use is permitted as part of an easement that the owners conveyed to the Chebeague and Cumberland Land Trust; the easement also restricts use of the field to agriculture, animal husbandry, and seasonal berry picking. The farmhouse and barns are not open to the public; visitors are asked to respect the privacy of the owners.

Directions & Parking: From the Chandler's Cove Landing follow the road from the wharf to South Rd. Turn left and then first right on South Shore Dr. A town right-of-way to the shore begins where the road curves to the right. Because parking is extremely limited, leave vehicles on South Rd. **Lat/Long:** 43.7160, -70.1194

30. Jenks Landing

The town-owned road provides access to a quiet stretch of sand and pebble beach located at the northeast end of Coleman Cove. Beach grass grows thickly just above the tide line; adjacent property – a few homes – is privately held. The beach looks out to Hope, Cliff and Sand Islands.

Directions & Parking: From the Casco Bay Lines Ferry landing, go out to South Rd and take a left. Take second right on Jenks Rd and follow to the end. Parking is limited, so park on South Rd. **Lat/Long:** 43.7180, -70.1151

31. Chandler Cove Beach

This easy-to-access, gorgeous curve of sand beach – tucked between two residential headlands – looks out onto lobster boats and recreational craft moored in the cove with Little Chebeague and Long Island beyond. It's a great place to swim and picnic. The town owns 300 feet of shoreline here with approximately 9 acres of upland that includes a stand of dune grass.

Directions & Parking: From the Chandler's Cove Landing follow the road from the wharf to South Rd. Turn left and go about 0.25 mile to a right-of-way sign on the left at Chandler Cove Field Rd. Follow a dirt road to the shore and park along the loop at the end. Two footpaths lead to the beach. **Lat/Long:** 43.7192, -70.1245

32. Ancient Burying Ground at the Belvin Property

Locally referred to as the Indian Burial Ground (although it's not certain that any Native Americans are buried here), this site has some 45 standing stones, all chiseled from island bedrock and all without inscriptions. The graves likely date from the 1700s to early 1800s. David Upton, an island patriot and veteran, rests at an unknown location. The modern granite markers delineate the presumed perimeter of the burial ground. The remainder of this property is not open to the public; visitors are asked to respect the owners' privacy.

Directions & Parking: Follow directions to the town-owned Chandler Cove Beach. From there, take a narrow path marked by a Chebeague and Cumberland Land Trust logo through the dune grass. To protect the dunes, which in turn protect the beach, do not stray from the path. **Lat/Long:** 43.7200, -70.1250

33. Indian Point Conservation Easement

The easement on this property provides limited access for pedestrians to cross a low-tide sandbar to Little Chebeague, which has 25 acres of superb birding habitat with 3,700 feet of shoreline. Visitors to Little Chebeague should be wary of several challenges: A powerful tide and undertow can wash across the bar; miscalculation of the tide can result in being stranded; Little Chebeague has stinging nettles, poison ivy, ticks and browntail moth. As with any conservation site, visitors to Indian Point may not cut or collect plants, as the area is extremely vulnerable to erosion; seashells and marine life should be left in place. Dogs are discouraged, especially during the migratory bird season; if taken, dogs must be leashed or under voice control. Only those with licenses from the Town of Chebeague may dig clams.

Directions & Parking: From Chandler's Cove Landing, go out to South Rd. Take a left and at first main road junction turn left on Cottage Rd. After the road curves north, take a left on Indian Point Rd (also known as 'the Hook'), a town dirt road that descends to the beach. Visitors are encouraged to walk to this area, as parking at the end of the road is limited. The dirt road that continues past the beach entrance and the tip of the point are both private; visitors are asked to remain on property included in the easement. **Lat/Long**: 43.7206, -70.1393

34. Sunset Road Right-of-Way 

This right-of-way is very much off the beaten path. The trail leads to a rocky ledge and minute pocket beach with a view to the west – the perfect place to watch the sunset.

Directions & Parking: From the Casco Bay Lines Ferry landing, go out to South Rd, take a left and go 0.5 mile until the road turns sharply to the right; take first left on School House Rd. Turn left at the "T" on North Rd and go 0.3 mile; Sunset Rd is the third road on the right. Park on the shoulder of North Rd. Walk about a thousand feet along Sunset Rd; when the road veers to the right, keep going straight on a path through the woods (another thousand feet) to the water. **Lat/Long:** 43.7266, -70.1391

Sunset Road

35. Waldo Point Right-of-Way 

This site, which commercial fishermen have used for boat access, leads to rocks and a small beach. It is possible to hand-carry and launch from the beach to explore the islands east of Chebeague.

Directions & Parking: Follow directions to Waldo Point, but bear left at the end of the road; parking is very limited. Take the grassy right-of-way to the shore.
Lat/Long: 43.7230, -70.1100

36. Waldo Point

This sand beach, which looks out onto Johnson Cove, offers access for clammers and provides others with a quiet place to commune with nature. The swimming, though possible, is not considered stellar. The front beach is narrow; the deep back beach is dotted with shells, driftwood, beach grass and sumacs.

Directions & Parking: From the Casco Bay Lines ferry landing, go out to South Rd and take a left. Go 0.25 mile and take the third right onto John Small Rd. Go almost a mile and turn right on Rose Point Rd. Go 0.3 mile and take a right at the "T." Follow the road to a mowed area straight ahead; park on the grass (very limited). Follow a path bearing right to the beach.
Lat/Long: 43.7230, -70.1110

37. Rose's Point Beach

Also known as Niblic Beach, this popular stretch of soft sand has been a favorite picnic spot for generations. It also offers good swimming and beach combing, despite the less-than-isolated location next to a marina. The strand is narrow, so the best time to show up is on a falling or low tide. To the south, the beach is bounded by beach grass and woods that protect a freshwater pond to the west. To the north, there are shrubs and private homes. Public access to the beach is protected under a conservation easement held by the Chebeague and Cumberland Land Trust; visitors are asked to carry out all trash.

Directions & Parking: From the Casco Bay Lines Ferry landing, go out to South Rd and take a left. Go 0.25 mile and take the third right on John Small Rd. Go almost a mile to a boatyard on the right. Park on the road; take the wide town path along the boatyard to the shore.
Lat/Long: 43.7292, -70.1110

38. Central Landing Road Right-of-Way 

This small beach, with more small rocks than sand, provides views eastward of Goose Nest, Crow, Bangs, and Stockman Islands. Generations of fishermen have used this site to reach their moored boats.

Directions & Parking: From the Casco Bay Lines Ferry landing, go out to South Rd and take a left. Go almost 2 miles to Wharf Rd, a grassy path to the shore on the right. Park along the South Rd and walk a short distance to the water. **Lat/Long:** 43.7365, 70.1074

39. Fenderson Road Right-of-Way

This small, rocky outcrop provides access for commercial fishermen and the public; it's also a good place for a picnic.

Directions & Parking: From the Casco Bay Lines Ferry landing, go out to South Rd and take a left. Travel north about 2.5 miles. Turn left on Fenderson Rd and follow it to the end. This is a privately-owned working waterfront. All fishing related gear should be left undisturbed. Parking is extremely limited. Walk along the mowed area to the water.
Lat/Long: 43.7408, -70.1034

40. Soule Road Right-of-Way

This right-of-way leads to a beach – more rock than sand – that looks east to Whaleboat Island and Harpswell Neck.

Directions & Parking: From the Casco Bay Lines Ferry landing, go out to South Rd and take a left. Go 3 miles to the north end of the island and turn right on Soule Rd, just past the golf course, following it to the end. Park on South Rd. A mowed path leads through trees and shrubs to steps that go down to the water. **Lat/Long:** 43.7520, -70.0982

41. The Gray Path

This diminutive easement, held by the Chebeague and Cumberland Land Trust, provides the only public access to the beach at the East End. For visitors landing at the Stone Wharf, it offers a pleasant walk with an old stone wall on one side and private gardens on the other. The path crosses a marshy area, where a boardwalk allows access even in the wettest season. Kayakers may land at this beach and use the path to reach South Road. Only the path and the steps are open to the public; visitors are asked to remain on the path and respect the privacy of the owners.

Directions & Parking: From the Casco Bay Lines ferry landing, go out to South Rd and take a left. Go 3 miles to the north end of the island, then 0.3 mile past Stone Wharf Rd. An historic island house, called "Falmouth," lies where the road turns sharply to the right. A tree in the garden with a land trust logo marks the trailhead; more land trust badges delineate the width of the easement. **Lat/Long**: 43.7559, -70.0991

42. Stone Wharf

The Chebeague Transportation Company operates a ferry from Cousins Island that docks at the Stone Wharf, near the northwest tip of the island. There is also a paved, trailerable boat ramp; limited floats are available (for a fee) to tie up small boats. Anglers can fish from the wharf. Golfers appear as well, as one of the tees of the Great Chebeague Golf Course is located on the wharf.

Directions & Parking: The wharf is located at the end of Stone Wharf Rd at the north end of the island. Parking is restricted on the Stone Wharf in June and November when lobstermen are setting and taking up gear. Parking demand often exceeds space available.
Lat/Long: 43.7512, -70.1073

43. Division Point Right-of-Way

This 10-foot path leads across the lawn of a nearby house and down a wooden stairway to a small sand beach and 1500 feet of marshy shoreline suited to quiet recreation and clamming. The view looks west to Cousins Island and the mainland.

Directions & Parking: From the Casco Bay Lines Ferry landing, go out to South Rd and take a left. Go a little more than a mile and turn left on Littlefield Rd. Take road to North Rd and turn right. Take second left Division Point Rd. Go left onto Division Point Rd to the end and park on the shoulder. Follow the path straight to the water. **Lat/Long:** 43.7452, -70.1245

Division Point

Casco Bay Islands

The Guide includes sites on six of Casco Bay's inhabited islands – Peaks, Little and Great Diamond, Long, Cliff and Chebeague. All are accessible via the Casco Bay Lines ferry service from Maine State Pier on Commercial Street in Portland. Visitors must purchase separate tickets for bikes and dogs. Note that Chebeague Island is also served by the private Chebeague Transportation Company, which runs ferries from Yarmouth. For more information on ferry services, see their websites: www.cascobaylines.com and http://www.chebeaguetrans.com.

Keep in mind that the islands have limited public facilities for visitors, including restrooms, stores and bathrooms. It is a good idea to learn more information about the islands before visiting, either through the ferry websites or town websites (see Resources section).

On-Island Transportation:

As a short-term or day visitor to the islands, it is impractical and in some cases impossible to take a vehicle with you. Peaks Island is the only island to which there is a regularly scheduled car ferry, but given the size of the island and scarcity of parking, one would be better served by biking. Some islands, like the Diamonds and Cliff Island, are easily traversed by foot due to their size and geography.

For Peaks Island, Long Island and Chebeague Island, bicycles (welcome on all the islands) are an excellent way to explore; Peaks Island even has two bike rental operations are located near the ferry dock.

As a pedestrian or biker on the islands, keep in mind that you might be sharing the road with automobiles or golf carts. While most roads are named, they are not necessarily marked. All of these factors make planning ahead, and carrying a map, essential to an enjoyable visit.

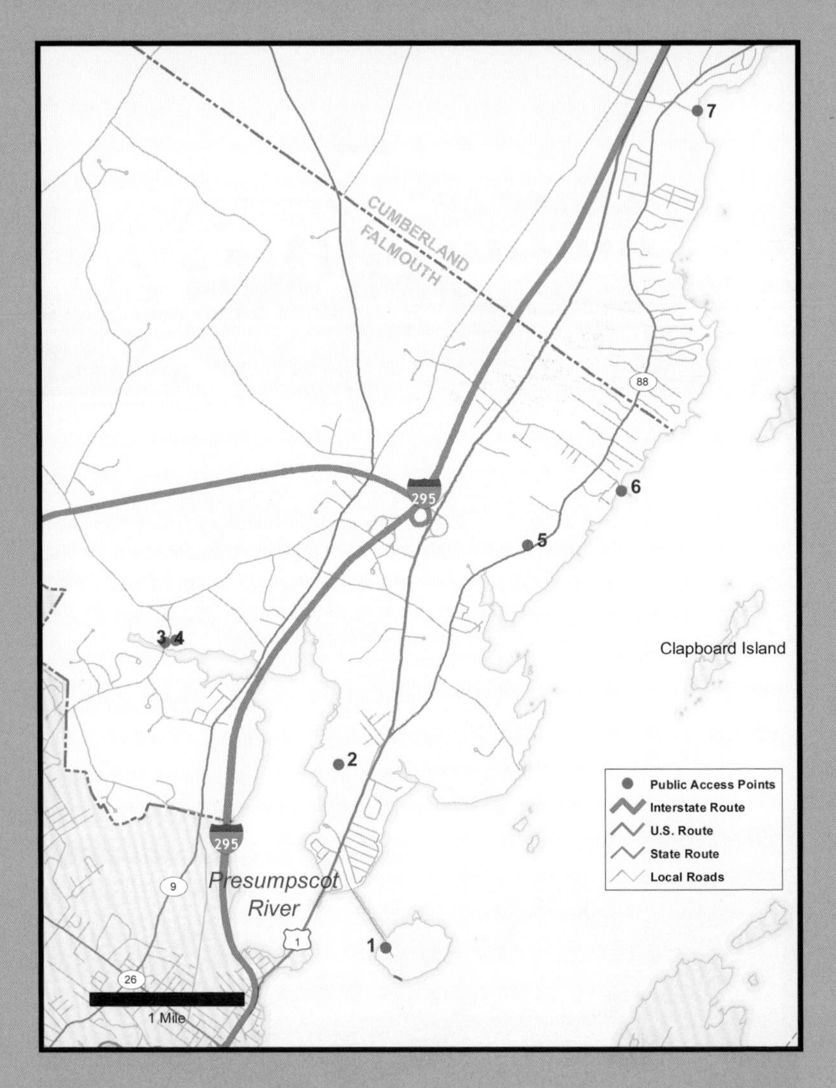

Falmouth-Cumberland

1. Mackworth Island State Park
2. Gilsland Farm
3. Walton Park
4. Presumpscot Falls Park
5. Falmouth Nature Preserve
6. Falmouth Town Landing
7. Town Landing

Falmouth-Cumberland

1. Mackworth Island State Park

A 1.25-mile trail circumnavigates this 100-acre state-owned island. The view changes at every curve: Going counter-clockwise, visitors first see the mainland, then Fort Gorges (the flat-topped stone structure), Little Diamond, Great Diamond, Cow, Clapboard and other more distant islands. The wide, generally hard-packed dirt trail with a gentle slope goes through pine, hemlock and oak woodland. Side trails can be steeper, and the main trail can be slippery when wet. At leisurely pace, the trail takes about an hour. Birders or those who follow side trails to the shore water – pockets of sand and cobble, or ledge – should plan extra time. The interior of the island is not open to the public. An entrance fee is charged.

Directions & Parking: Take I-295 to exit 9. Turn north onto Route 1, go 0.8 mile, turn right on Andrews Ave, continue over the causeway, and park in the lot on the right.
Lat/Long: 43.6892, -70.2351

2. Gilsland Farm

This 65-acre sanctuary along the Presumpscot River is the headquarters for Maine Audubon. From dawn to dusk, year-round, visitors may walk, snowshoe, or ski along the gentle trails that wind through meadows, woods and salt marsh, skirting a pond and tidal mud flats. Observation platforms and blinds are located at key viewing spots. The area supports many birds, mammals, butterflies and dragonflies. The peony display in June provides a particular treat. The main building houses exhibits, a "Discovery Room" for children, a nature store and a resource center for teachers. Maine Audubon offers many programs, year-round. Pets and bikes are not allowed.

Directions & Parking: Take I-295 to exit 9. Go 1.9 miles north on Route 1; turn left on Gilsland Farm Rd at the Maine Audubon sign just before the intersection with ME 88. Park in the large lot.
Lat/Long: 43.7064, -70.2415

3. Walton Park

This site provides visitors with an old-fashioned swimming hole on the Presumpscot River. A wide, smooth trail laid out in switchbacks leads downhill. A three-tiered set of wooden steps connects the trail to a ramp and float – the perfect place to rest between laps or dry out in the sun. At low tide, a bar forms on the other side of the river, providing another place to enjoy the view. Although it is possible to hand-carry a kayak, it's a long way down and the trip seems even longer when it's time to haul back up the steep hill.

Directions & Parking: Follow directions to Presumpscot Falls Park. Pull off on the opposite side of the road into a small lot. **Lat/Long:** 43.7179, -70.2631

Walton Park

4. Presumpscot Falls Park 

Visitors can follow a trail on the north shore through mixed woods – on a sunny day, reflected light from overhanging trees can turn the water a shimmering, translucent green – to a viewpoint of the tidal falls. The Smelt Hill Dam, once located here, was removed in 2002 to enhance the river's fishery, allowing anadromous species such as shad and river herring upstream access. Fishermen particularly like this section of the Presumpscot, angling for striped bass. Portland Trails purchased this land in 2002. Please respect private property west of the falls.

Directions & Parking: From I-295 north, take exit 6B and go north on ME 100/US 302/Forest Ave. Go 2.5 miles, bear left onto Allen, and go 2.6 miles. On the other side of the bridge, pull into off-road parking. **Lat/Long:** 43.7175, -70.2644

5. Falmouth Nature Preserve 

The trails here wind through hemlock, yellow and white birch, beech and maple. They connect with paths in the adjacent Mill Creek Preserve (owned by Falmouth Land Trust), which does not have its own road access. Together these preserves offer 100 acres of splendid hiking, snowshoeing and cross-country skiing. Both have stream frontage, and both offer opportunities to watch birds (especially warblers in spring), identify flowers, and listen to the leaves rustle in the breeze. Pets must be leashed.

Directions & Parking: From the intersection of Johnson and Foreside Rds, go 0.7 mile south on ME 88/Foreside Rd and turn down a dirt road that lies directly opposite 177 Foreside. Park along the dirt road**. Lat/Long:** 43.7276, -70.2169

6. Falmouth Town Landing

This part-tide paved ramp, pier with floats, and small sand beach is all but dedicated to town residents. If others can find parking, they may also launch (fee), wade in the water, take in the view to Sturdivant, Basket, and Clapboard Islands, and enjoy the narrow ribbon of sand. Both commercial fishermen and recreational boaters use the landing regularly, and there are many moorings just off shore. A general store is stationed at the top of the hill.

Directions & Parking: From Falmouth, go north on Route 1 and turn right onto Johnson Rd. At the intersection with Foreside Rd, go straight onto Town Landing Rd. Parking is by permit only at the landing and mostly by permit at lot on Foreside Rd. Seasonal on-street parking is available in front of Underwood Park, nearby. **Lat/Long:** 43.7325, -70.2049

Falmouth Town Landing

7. Town Landing

This site on Broad Cove looks out to Prince Point and Casco Bay. Most people simply enjoy the view, but it is possible to hand-carry down the metal steps and put in from ledge. At high tide, the water is about a foot and a half deep; a falling tide reveals a mud flat – perfect for digging clams, other shellfish and marine worms – but mucky for paddlers.

Directions & Parking: From Yarmouth, go south on ME 88 and turn left onto Town Landing Rd near the King's Highway Road. Continue to the small, circular parking area.
Lat/Long: 43.7682, -70.1955

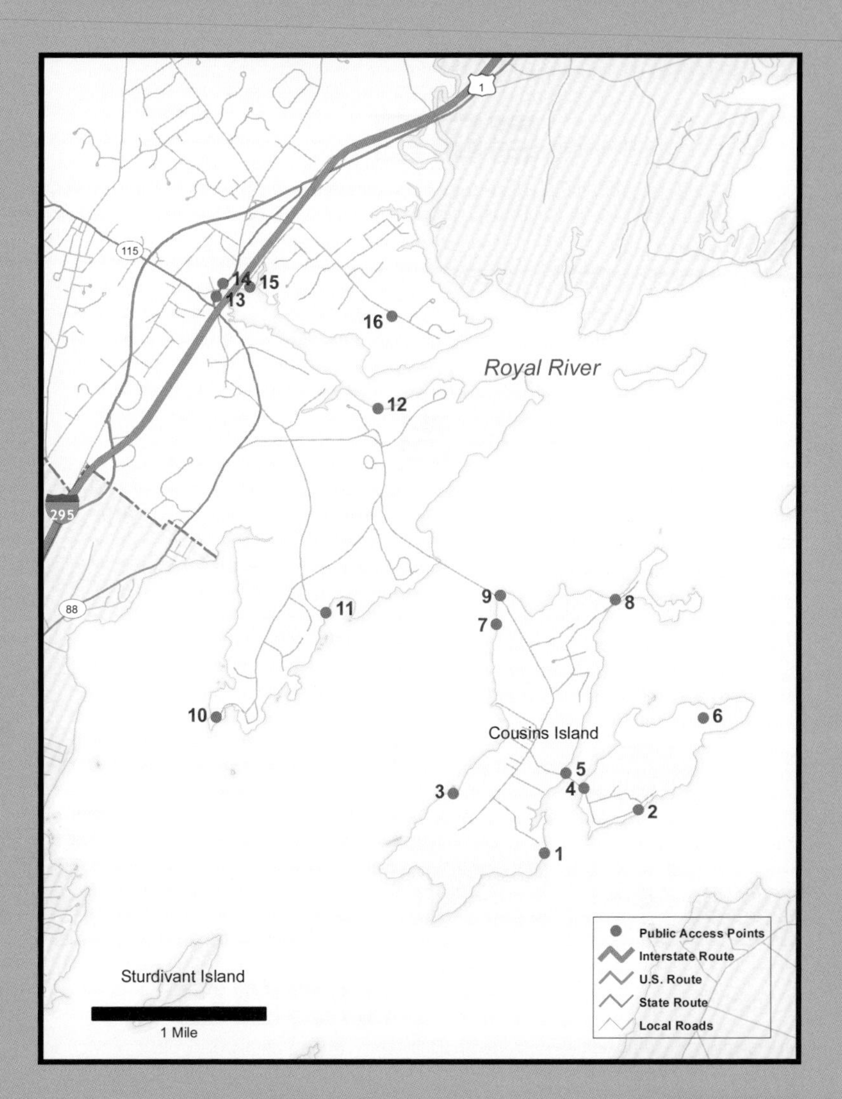

Yarmouth

1. Cousins Island Dock
2. Littlejohn Island Town Dock
3. Madeline Point on Cousins Island
4. Littlejohn Narrows Overlook
5. Talbot Road Right-of-Way on Cousins Island
6. Littlejohn Island Preserve
7. Camp SOCI
8. Sea Meadows Lane
9. Sandy Point Beach on Cousins Island
10. Sunset Point Overlook
11. Old Town Landing
12. Larrabee's Landing
13. Gendall Memorial
14. Grist Mill Park
15. Town Landing
16. Spear Farm Estuary Preserve

Yarmouth

1. Cousins Island Dock

The Chebeague Transportation Company's ferry to Chebeague Island operates from this dock. There are also some floats for small boats; larger boats are moored just offshore.

Directions & Parking: From Cousins Island, take Cousins St and turn left onto Wharf Rd. Follow Wharf to its end (a very tight area with no parking), drop off passengers or boat, and then back-track to the parking lot located just up the street. Ferry passengers can check the ferry's website for information about the satellite lot on Route 1 in Cumberland; a bus conveys patrons to the dock. **Lat/Long:** 43.7520, -70.1398

2. Littlejohn Island Town Dock

The town provides a dock, ramp and seasonal float with tie-ups. Moorings for larger boats are just offshore. The parcel is a favored site for bluefish and striper fishing; and children (and adults) can explore the pools that form during the lower half of the tide.

Directions & Parking: The dock is located about half a mile from the causeway, on Littlejohn Rd. Parking is very limited and for residents only from late spring to early winter. Others are advised to park at the causeway and walk to the dock. Parking is not allowed at night.
Lat/Long: 43.7557, -70.1290

Littlejohn Island Town Dock

3. Madeline Point on Cousins Island

The town dock, ramp and float, which lie north of the Wyman Station power plant, provide access to a public mooring area between Cousins Island and the mainland. A small shingle beach runs between the dock and a scenic outcrop – "Contemplation Rock" – that visitors use to bask in the sun or take in the view. Paddlers can hand launch from the beach. Swimmers enjoy the warmish, protected water in the cove.

Directions & Parking: Cross the bridge from the mainland and follow Cousins St to the Madeline Point Rd/Wharf Rd crossroads. Turn right onto Madeline, then a left at the "V." Parking is allowed at designated spots, some reserved for commercial fishermen, at the end of the road.
Lat/Long: 43.7569, -70.1504

4. Littlejohn Narrows Overlook

Herons, egrets, eiders, black ducks, ospreys, kingfishers and many other birds frequent this tidal stretch that is sometimes water, sometimes mud, between Cousins and Littlejohn Islands. In migration, shorebirds forage along the shore. The keen-eyed visitor may also spot mink, raccoon, and other mammal tracks where land interfaces with water. Boaters can hand-carry, being mindful of the tidal restraint.

Directions & Parking: The overlook is on the right, just past the east end of the causeway from Cousins Island and across from Winter St. Parking along the road is very limited.
Lat/Long: 43.7575, -70.1355

5. Talbot Road Right-of-Way on Cousins Island

This right-of-way provides clammers access to flats between Cousins Island and Littlejohn. Parking is not allowed at night.

Directions & Parking: From the bridge onto Cousins Island, go a little more than a mile; turn left onto Talbot Rd. This site is on the left, just before the causeway to Littlejohn, with very limited parking along the north side of road. A path leads to clam flats.
Lat/Long: 43.7587, -70.1374

6. Littlejohn Island Preserve 

A half-mile loop trail hugs the coast, providing fine views of Cousins Island to the west, Little Mosher and Mosher Islands to the northeast, and Whaleboat and Great Chebeague to the east. The trail is largely dry and well maintained, but contains split logs and parallel-plank bridges that require balance and shoes with traction. Launching kayaks is not suitable or allowed; paddlers may launch elsewhere and visit the property for a daytime picnic, using a natural landing spot as all docks are private. Leashed or voice controlled dogs are allowed; owners absolutely must remove waste. Hunting is allowed, but only some forms are suitable and safe on this 23-acre property. Interested individuals should contact the Royal River Conservation Trust, which owns the preserve, for more information.

Directions & Parking: From Cousins Island, take Talbot Rd left onto Littlejohn Island. Take the second left, then the first left onto Pemasong Ln. Follow this dirt road to the end, passing through the Littlejohn Shores entrance gate; park at designated area (extremely limited) on left before the road becomes private. Walk 0.2 mile on the road to the preserve's trail.
Lat/Long: 43.7634, -70.1217

Littlejohn Island Preserve

7. Camp SOCI

Located on Cousins Island, this lovely wooded parcel includes an amphitheater with a small pavilion and tables (perfect for a picnic); a trail through mature oak and pine to the top of a bluff (for a bit of exercise); and a long flight of steps down to the water, where at mid- or low-water explorers can follow the shore north under the bridge to Sandy Point Beach. The view is west across the water to Princes Point on the mainland. During songbird migration, birders visit here regularly, scouting for elusive species among the regulars. The bluff is fragile and easily prone to erosion; visitors should remain on the trail or walk along the water. Various groups, including art camps and the Maine Conservation Corps, frequently reserve and use this property; other visitors are asked to respect their privacy. (Reservations can be made by contacting the Yarmouth Community Services.) SOCI is an acronym for Scouts On Cousins Island.

Directions & Parking: From Yarmouth, take Gilman Rd/Cousins St to Cousins Island. Cross the Snodgrass Bridge and park in the lot on the left as for Sandy Point Beach. Cross Cousins St to steps and a path. **Lat/Long:** 43.7728, -70.1453

8. Sea Meadows Lane

Many recreational clammers take advantage of this access to clam flats at the north end of Cousins Island. Other visitors may prefer to stop when the tide is higher, but should be aware that it's less a place to walk (that is, slurp in the mud) and more of a place to sit and observe. At high water, only the stone steps are exposed.

Directions & Parking: Cross the bridge from the mainland to Cousins Island and go 0.7 mile. Make a sharp left onto Sea Meadows Ln and continue to the white gate, which marks the end of the public road. Park on the left and descend the steps. **Lat/Long:** 43.7731, -70.1319

9. Sandy Point Beach on Cousins Island 

This beach, in the shadow of the Snodgrass Bridge, is a perennial family favorite, as young children can wade in the shallows and older children can swim in deeper water. Swimmers prefer to visit during the lower part of the tide because there is more beach area exposed; at high water, there's only a narrow strip of sand. Paddlers can hand-carry here, but must remember that low tide exposes a long sand bar that can lengthen the carry considerably. Clamming (with license) is permitted on exposed mud flats.

Directions & Parking: Cross the bridge from the mainland to Cousins Island; turn into an unpaved lot on the left. Follow the path a short distance to the beach. **Lat/Long:** 43.7733, -70.1452

Sandy Point Beach on Cousins Island

10. Sunset Point Overlook 

Despite the point's name, the view from here – lovely though it is – looks east to Cousins Island and south to Sturdivant Island, so it's better for a sunrise than sunset. Paddlers may hand-carry to the water; those with a small boat on a trailer can launch on a part-tide, unimproved gravel ramp.

Directions & Parking: From Yarmouth, go south on ME 88; 0.6 mile past I-295, veer left on Princes Point Rd and follow it to the end of the peninsula, bearing right when the road splits. At the crossroads with Sunset Point Rd and Battery Point Ln, park in the tiny lot on the lane. Walk a quarter of a mile along Sunset Point Rd to the overlook, which has no parking.
Lat/Long: 43.7627, -70.1778

11. Old Town Landing 

This small pebble beach, historically a town landing, now offers a place to hand-launch a boat or go for a swim (high tide recommended) in a protected cove. The flat rocks provide the perfect counterpoint to a refreshing swim. Children of all ages can explore the tide pools that form at low water, when a bar extends from shore to a cluster of rocks. Birders are attracted by various species of wading birds and coastal waterfowl. The landing is a lovely destination for those on bicycles, who can easily pack a lunch and towel, cycle to the site, and enjoy the water without concern about parking. The launch area is unsuitable for trailers, as it is not hard-packed and the access road is steep and narrow.

Directions & Parking: From the intersection of Princes Point, Morton, and Old Town Landing Rds in Yarmouth, go 0.3 mile southeast on Old Town Landing to very restricted parking on north side of road. The intertidal zone, though tempting as a parking area, floods at high tide.
Lat/Long: 43.7717, -70.1654

12. Larrabee's Landing 

A mowed path runs next to a split rail fence and through the woods about 400 feet to the river, where there was formerly a boat landing on the southwest shore of the Royal River estuary. Birders enjoy the opportunity to see species that frequent the river corridor; walkers like the pleasant stroll with a view at the end; bikers consider it a pretty spot to take a break.

Directions & Parking: From Yarmouth, go south on ME 88 over the Royal River bridge. From I-295 go 0.6 mile, turn left on Princes Point Rd, and take the second left onto Gilman Rd. Go 0.4 mile, turn left onto Larrabee Landing Rd, then left onto Burbank Ln. Park on-street.
Lat/Long: 43.7886, -70.1597

13. Gendall Memorial P

This postage-stamp sized park, mostly screened from the river by pines and maples, is the site of a memorial to Captain Walter Gendall, who ran a grist mill and saw mill at the falls in Yarmouth and who died near here while protecting settlers under attack during King William's War in 1688.

Directions & Parking: From Yarmouth, go south on ME 88/Main St over the Royal River bridge, then veer left onto Lafayette. Immediately pull over into a gravel lot on the left.
Lat/Long: 43.7977, -70.1787

14. Grist Mill Park 

Travelers driving I-295 can see First Falls, where the Royal River pours into tidal water, but it's a fleeting view. Those who visit Grist Mill Park can stand on old granite cribwork and watch as the water leaps and flows, slides over smooth ledge, and makes eddies and rooster tails at the bottom. The view is even more dramatic after a storm, when the Royal is swollen with runoff. Visitors can picnic at this former mill site (see the Gendall Memorial description), but most come to view the river.

Directions & Parking: From Yarmouth, go north on ME 88/Main St over the Royal River bridge; park immediately, on left. A path leads to the river. **Lat/Long**: 43.7988, -70.1779

15. Town Landing 

Although this busy site does include a small park, the main focus here is providing access to the harbor and the 2-mile Royal River estuary, a conduit to Casco Bay. The facilities include an all-tide launch ramp (fee) plus a set of floats for commercial fishermen and another for recreational boaters. At low tide this section of river, which is just below the head-of-tide falls, is quite narrow. An outhouse is located next to the parking lot. There is a fee to launch.

Directions & Parking: From Yarmouth, go north on ME 88 (which becomes Spring St) and go right on Bayview St. Take the first right onto Old Shipyard Rd and follow it to a lot at the end.
Lat/Long: 43.7986, -70.1748

16. Spear Farm Estuary Preserve 

This local treasure offers hikers, bird-watchers and nature-lovers more than 2 miles of trails on 48 acres of diverse habitat leading down to the Royal River. The climax oak and pine woods, bluffs, salt marsh, earthen dam, and pond overlook are prime birding sites. A kiosk at the lot and five interpretive signs on the trail offer habitat information. Cross-country skiers and snowshoers frequent the area in winter; the pond is available (although unmaintained) for skating in winter. A portion of trail lies on private property; visitors should respect posted signs. Dogs must be leashed; bikes are not permitted on trails.

Directions & Parking: From ME 88/E Main in Yarmouth, go north; veer right on ME 88/Spring St and take a right on Bayview St. Cross I-295 and go 0.9 mile. Turn right into a parking area in front of a barn. **Lat/Long:** 43.7963, -70.1582

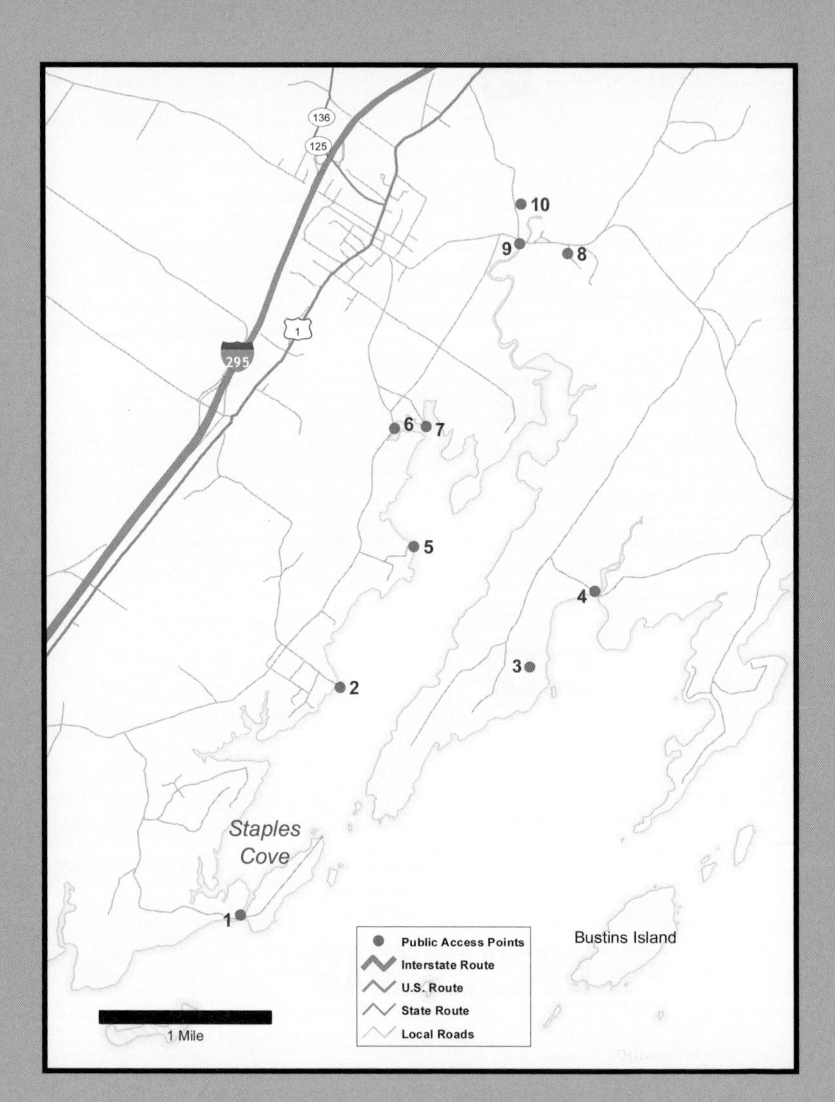

Freeport

1. Winslow Park and Campground
2. Town of Freeport Public Landing
3. Wolfe's Neck Woods State Park
4. Little River Access Point
5. Sandy Beach
6. Dunning Boat Yard
7. Porters Landing
8. Pettingill Farm Museum
9. Mill Stream Landing
10. Mast Landing Audubon Sanctuary

Freeport

1. Winslow Park and Campground

This multiple-use area has a paved, part-tide boat ramp (fee) and float; "part-tide" means that when the tide goes out, there's nothing but mud flats remaining. Clammers, paddlers, sailors and motor-boaters all launch here, and they are headed from Little River Bay south along Wolfe Neck to Casco Bay. Just past the launch is a gate to the park (fee), which offers something for everyone: a fishing pier, extensive picnic area, campsites, half-mile nature trail, and small sandy beach dedicated to swimming (boats are not allowed at the beach). Dogs must be leashed and may not be taken on the beach or playground.

Directions & Parking: From exit 17 on I-295, take Route 1 north. Turn right on South Freeport Rd, then right onto Staples Point Rd and go to its end. The parking lot for the boat launch is located outside the campground gate; other parking lots are sited inside.
Lat/Long: 43.8014, -70.1169

2. Town of Freeport Public Landing

This public wharf and dock across from the southern tip of Wolfe Neck provide commercial and recreational boats with deepwater access. Some people fish from the dock, but most users are headed for Casco Bay. Paddlers are advised to launch at quieter locales; this is a bustling harbor. A marina, lobster pound and restaurants are located nearby.

Directions & Parking: From Main St in Freeport, go south on Bow St. At the second right, turn onto South St and go 2.5 miles. Turn left onto Main St and follow to a parking area – very busy and likely to be full – at the end. **Lat/Long:** 43.8204, -70.1057

3. Wolfe's Neck Woods State Park

The 218-acre park offers five miles of lovely trails through white pine and hemlock, with views of Little River Bay and the Harraseeket River. Visitors can drop down to a salt marsh or skirt a small bog, but they are never far from the crumpled bedrock along the shore that separates land from sea. Googins Island, long the site for nesting ospreys, is a perennial crowd-pleaser. The park (fee charged) is open year-round, so visitors may hike, ski and snowshoe here in winter.

Directions & Parking: From Main St in Freeport, take Bow St south for one mile, turn right on Flying Point Rd and continue for 1.3 miles, then turn right onto Wolf Neck Rd. Continue to the park entrance on the left and a parking area. In winter, park along Wolf Neck Rd.
Lat/Long: 43.8223, -70.0835

Wolfe's Neck Woods State Park

4. Little River Access Point 

This site immediately east of Wolfe Neck provides water access to the small cove in which the Little River empties; beyond lies Casco Bay. At low water, clammers use the site regularly to reach the mud flats that support their livelihood. With enough water, paddlers who hand-carry can launch, but the site can be quite muddy. People also swim here when the tide is high. With plenty of water, it's possible to explore about half a mile upstream on the narrow river, but mostly paddlers head south to explore the bay's islands.

Directions & Parking: From Main St in Freeport, take Bow St south for one mile, turn right on Flying Point Rd and continue for 1.3 miles, then turn right onto Wolf Neck Rd and go 1.7 miles. Turn left on Burnett and go 0.3 mile. Access is on the west side of the bridge, where there is limited parking on the shoulder. **Lat/Long:** 43.8287, -70.0760

5. Sandy Beach 

This small town-owned beach doesn't see much activity, which means that those who do visit enjoy a bit of solitude. The strip of sand is narrow, partly vegetated, and shaded in the afternoon. Clammers use the site to gain access to flats; fishermen come to cast a line; area residents enjoy the opportunity to get down to the water for a view of the Harraseeket River and Wolf Neck. It is possible but challenging to hand-carry a boat down the steep set of steps.

Directions & Parking: From Main St in Freeport, go south on Bow St. At the second right, turn onto South St and go 1.8 miles. Turn left on Cushing Briggs Rd and continue to very limited parking at the end. **Lat/Long:** 43.8321, -70.0973

6. Dunning Boat Yard Ramp

This concrete public ramp, located next to Dunning Boat Yard, provides access to the upper Harraseeket River, which then empties into the northern end of the harbor. Paddlers and those with small motor craft must plan their excursions for the top half of the tide because the area all but drains at low tide.

Directions & Parking: From Main St in Freeport, go south on South Freeport Rd to the boat yard. Park on the pullout on the left, where there are some trailer spots.
Lat/Long: 43.8419, -70.0100

7. Porters Landing

At this part-tide landing, paddlers launch from a dock rather than a ramp. Marsh and pines line the shore to the south; the upper reaches of Freeport's harbor lie in the distance. Clammers and the occasional boater use the site, which is also a scenic spot to sit on the dock and enjoy the peace and quiet. The landing is open sunrise to sunset, with no overnight parking or boat tie-up. Visitors must carry in/carry out.

Directions & Parking: From Main St in Freeport, take Bow St south; at the second right turn onto South St and follow it for almost a mile. Turn left onto Lower Mast Landing Rd, then take an immediate right onto Cove Rd. Follow to a tiny turn-around with very limited parking.
Lat/Long: 43.8422, -70.0960

Porters Landing

8. Pettingill Farm Museum

This museum and surrounding land on the Harraseeket River are a classic example of an 1800s salt-water farm. Visitors may stroll along 3.5 miles of trail that traverse 140 acres of fields, woods, gardens, orchard (with antique apple and cherry trees) and salt marsh. It's a magnificent place to spread out a blanket and hold a picnic – as long as the wind is blowing or you are armed with repellent, for the mosquitoes at times can be fierce in summer. The public is welcome year-round, dawn until dusk. The Freeport Historical Society opens the house, a salt box with huge center chimney, only by appointment or during Pettingill Farm Days in spring and fall. The last Pettingill lived here until 1970; the building never had electricity or plumbing.

Directions & Parking: From Main St in Freeport, take Bow St south for 1.5 miles, turn right onto Pettingill Rd, go a short distance, and park at the gate on the left. A 15-minute walk along the dirt road (with private property on each side) leads to the farmhouse.
Lat/Long: 43.8567, -70.0797

9. Mill Stream Landing

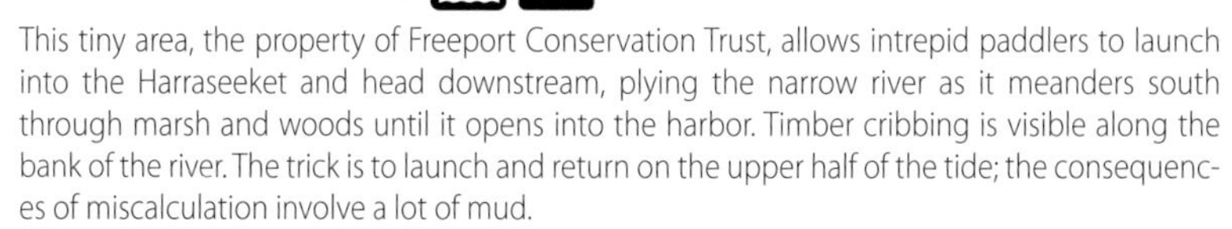

This tiny area, the property of Freeport Conservation Trust, allows intrepid paddlers to launch into the Harraseeket and head downstream, plying the narrow river as it meanders south through marsh and woods until it opens into the harbor. Timber cribbing is visible along the bank of the river. The trick is to launch and return on the upper half of the tide; the consequences of miscalculation involve a lot of mud.

Directions & Parking: From Main St in Freeport, take Bow St south for one mile. Opposite Upper Mast Landing Rd, pull over in a paved area with very limited parking and carry to the water.
Lat/Long: 43.8575, -70.0854

Mast Landing Audubon Sanctuary

10. Mast Landing Audubon Sanctuary

For years, Maine Audubon held a summer camp for children here at the head of the Harraseeket River, so visitors can be assured that there's lots to see. The 140-acre parcel has 3.5 miles of trails that snake through fields and a mature pine/hemlock forest, skirting salt marsh, orchard, freshwater stream, alder lowland, and the foundation of an old mill.
Birders cruise the trails for songbirds and migrant shorebirds. The sanctuary is also a lovely area to observe the American woodcock's annual spring courtship display: The male circles upward and then plummets to the ground, where it utters a succinct "Beep!" Although mammals are generally secretive, the prints of porcupine, mink, fisher and deer can sometimes be found on a snowy trail or in mud along the stream.

Directions & Parking: From Main St in Freeport, take Bow St south for one mile and turn left on Upper Mast Landing Rd. Go a short distance and turn right at the sign; park in lot at the top of the hill. **Lat/Long:** 43.8607, -70.0852

Maine Coastal Program

Balancing the conservation and sustainable development of Maine's coastal resources & coastal communities

Coastweek – *A Celebration of Maine's Coast*

Each September, in celebration of Maine's coastal resources, local groups from Kittery to Calais sponsor outings, lectures, events and – the premier activity – Coastal Cleanup. For more than 30 years, on the second Saturday of September and in the days following, volunteers – residents and visitors, children and adults, school groups and civic organizations – collect, recycle and dispose of thousands of pounds of trash. They carefully record the volume, location and type of debris, with the goal that the information can, at some point, be used to eliminate trash at its source. For many individuals, Coastal Cleanup is their first exposure to marine issues as well as first volunteer activity; some of them become lifelong stewards.

Trash on the shore is unsightly and smelly, but more importantly it threatens wildlife. Fish, sea turtles, birds and marine mammals can ingest or choke on debris or become fatally entangled in rope. Products and packaging are buoyant and resistant to breaking down, so they can travel for years and wash up on shorelines even in remote locations.

Maine's effort is part of the Ocean Conservancy's International Coastal Cleanup, which involves more than 150 states and countries. The nonprofit organization maintains a database and produces an annual report with telling figures. In 2009, for example, 60 percent of the debris was disposable, single-use items including more than a million plastic bags and enough cups, plates and utensils for a picnic for 100,000 people.

For details about Maine's Coastweek, information about how to become a coastal steward and cleanup registration material, visit **www.mainecoastalprogram.org.** Or, contact the program coordinator at 207-287-2351.

Acknowledgments

The *Guide* would not have been possible without the assistance of 130 Maine towns and cities and more than 40 land trusts that provided site information and carefully reviewed site descriptions. The Maine Coastal Program offers its deepest gratitude to participating local government and land trust staff.

The Maine Coastal Public Access Guide project development team included:

- Julia Noordyk, National Oceanic and Atmospheric Administration Coastal Management Fellow - Project Manager, Co-editor
- Melissa Anson, Maine Coastal Program – Assistant Project Manager, Field Staff
- Matthew Nixon, Maine Coastal Program – Project Coordinator
- Kathleen Leyden, Maine Coastal Program, and Paul Dest, Wells National Estuarine Research Reserve – Co-editors
- Dorcas S. Miller, Freelance Writer and Editorial Consultant – Principal Author
- Randall Landry, Graphic Design and Marketing Consultant – Design and Layout
- Bill Duffy, Northern Geomantics – Cartographic Design
- Catherine Johnston and Justin Schlawin, Maine Natural Areas Program, and Erin Quigley, Kingfisher Conservation & Recreation LLC – Map Production
- Matthew Brooks, Michael Giudilli, Ethan Noordyk and Ethan Pierce – Field Staff
- Penmor Lithographers – Printing

Project Advisory Committee:

- George Powell, Maine Department of Agriculture, Conservation and Forestry
- Brian Marcaurelle, Maine Island Trail Association
- Bruce Joule, Maine Department of Marine Resources
- Leon Bucher, Maine Department of Inland Fisheries and Wildlife
- Kristen Grant, University of Maine Sea Grant College Program

Production of the *Guide* was funded by the National Oceanic and Atmospheric Administration's Office of Ocean and Coastal Resource Management, NOAA's Coastal Services Center, the Maine Outdoor Heritage Fund and the Department of Agriculture, Conservation and Forestry, Division of Parks and Public Lands.

Resources

Participating Nonprofit Organizations

Biddeford Pool Land Trust
Website: N/A • Phone: N/A
Email: tcbplme@yahoo.com

Chebeague & Cumberland Land Trust
Website: www.ccltmaine.org
Phone: 207-699-2989
Email: info@ccltmaine.org

Falmouth Land Trust
Website: www.falmouthlandtrust.org
Phone: 207-797-9728
Email: info@falmouthlandtrust.org

Freeport Conservation Trust
Website: www.freeportconservationtrust.org
Phone: 207-865-3985 ext. 212
Email: info@freeportconservationtrust.org

Great Works Regional Land Trust
Website: www.gwrlt.org
Phone: 207-646-3604
Email: info@gwrlt.org

Kennebunk Land Trust
Website: www.kennebunklandtrust.org
Phone: 207-985-7649
Email: info@kennebunklandtrust.org

Kennebunkport Conservation Trust
Website: www.kporttrust.org
Phone: 207-967-3465
Email: tom@kctoffice.com

Kittery Land Trust
Website: www.kitterylandtrust.org
Phone: 207-439-8989
Email: info@kitterylandtrust.org

Maine Audubon
Website: www.maineaudubon.org
Phone: 207-781-2330
Email: info@maineaudubon.org

Maine Coast Heritage Trust
Website: www.mcht.org
Phone: 207-729-7366
Email: info@mcht.org

Oceanside Conservation Trust of Casco Bay
Website: www.oceansideconservationtrust.org
Phone: 207-699-2989
Email: conservationcollaborative@gmail.com

Peaks Island Land Preserve
Website: www.preservepeaks.org
Phone: N/A
Email: pilp@mainecoastguide.com

Portland Trails
Website: www.trails.org
Phone: 207-775-2411
Email: info@trails.org

Royal River Conservation Trust
Website: www.rrct.org
Phone: 207-847-9399
Email: info@RRCT.org

Saco Bay Trails
Website: www.sacobaytrails.org
Phone: 207-286-9295
Email: info@sacobaytrails.org

South Portland Land Trust
Website: www.southportlandlandtrust.org
Phone: N/A
Email: sopolandtrust@gmail.com

The Nature Conservancy
Website: www.nature.org/maine
Phone: 207-729-5181
Email: naturemaine@tnc.org

York Land Trust
Website: www.yorklandtrust.org
Phone: 207-363-7400
Email: info@yorklandtrust.org

Participating Cities & Towns

Biddeford
Website: www.biddefordmaine.org
Phone: 207-284-9307

Cape Elizabeth
Website: www.capeelizabeth.com
Phone: 207-799-5251

Chebeague Island
Website: www.townofchebeagueisland.org
Phone: 207-846-3148

Cumberland
Website: www.cumberlandmaine.com
Phone: 207-829-5559

Eliot
Website: www.eliotmaine.org
Phone: 207-439-1813

Falmouth
Website: www.town.falmouth.me.us
Phone: 207-781-5253

Freeport
Website: www.freeportmaine.com
Phone: 207-865-4743

Kennebunk
Website: www.kennebunkmaine.us
Phone: 207-985-2102

Kennebunkport
Website: www.kennebunkportme.gov
Phone: 207-967-4243

Kittery
Website: www.kitteryme.gov
Phone: 207-439-0452

Long Island
Website: www.townoflongisland.us
Phone: 207-766-5820

Ogunquit
Website: www.townofogunquit.org
Phone: 207-646-5139

Old Orchard Beach
Website: www.oobmaine.com
Phone: 207-934-5714

Portland
Website: www.portlandmaine.gov
Phone: 207-874-8300

Saco
Website: www.sacomaine.org
Phone: 207-282-4191

Scarborough
Website: www.scarborough.me.us
Phone: 207-730-4000

South Berwick
Website: www.southberwickmaine.org
Phone: 207-384-3300

South Portland
Website: www.southportland.org
Phone: 207-767-3201

Wells
Website: www.wellstown.org
Phone: 207-646-5114

Yarmouth
Website: www.yarmouth.me.us
Phone: 207-846-9036

York
Website: www.yorkmaine.org
Phone: 207-363-1000

Participating State and Federal Agencies

Maine Department of Agriculture, Conservation and Forestry
Division of Parks and Public Lands
Website: www.maine.gov/doc/parks
Phone: 207-287-3821

Maine Department of Economic & Community Development • Maine Office of Tourism
Website: www.visitmaine.com
Phone: 1-888-624-6345

Maine Department of Inland Fisheries and Wildlife
Website: www.maine.gov/ifw
Phone: 207-287-8000

Maine Department of Marine Resources
Website: www.maine.gov/dmr
Phone: 207-624-6550

U.S. Department of Homeland Security
U.S. Coast Guard
Website: www.uscg.mil
Phone: 202-372-4620

U.S. Department of Interior
U.S. Fish and Wildlife Service
Rachel Carson National Wildlife Refuge
Website: www.fws.gov/refuge/rachel_carson
Phone: 207-646-9226

Wells National Estuarine Research Reserve
Website: www.wellsreserve.org
Phone: 207-646-1555

Disclaimers

The *Guide* is not inclusive of all public access sites on the Maine coast:

- Site information was collected in 2011 and 2012.
- Island sites reachable only by private boat were not included.
- Areas not yet ready for visitation, such as those without trails, were excluded.
- Based on recommendations from land managers, some sites containing very sensitive ecological features, prone to damage by heavy visitation, were not included.
- Some sites may have been inadvertently left out of this edition of the *Guide*.

Every effort has been made to provide accurate, current information (as of 2012). However, site status and ownership, signs, roads, ferry service, amenities, rules and other information may change. We welcome feedback, corrections and information about additional coastal access sites. Correspondence should be directed to:

Coastal Access Guide Manager
Maine Coastal Program
93 State House Station • Augusta, ME 04333
DCN.Info-MCP@Maine.gov
207-287-2801